Land Mines

Other titles in the Issues in Focus *series:*

ADVERTISING
Information or Manipulation?
ISBN 0-7660-1106-2

AIDS
An All-About Guide for Young Adults
ISBN 0-89490-716-6

AIR SAFETY
Preventing Future Disasters
ISBN 0-7660-1108-9

ALTERNATIVE MEDICINE
Is It for You?
ISBN 0-89490-955-X

ANIMAL EXPERIMENTATION
Cruelty or Science? Revised Edition
ISBN 0-7660-1244-1

CHEMICAL AND BIOLOGICAL WARFARE
The Cruelest Weapons, Revised Edition
ISBN 0-7660-1241-7

COMPUTER CRIME
Phreaks, Spies, and Salami Slicers, Revised Edition
ISBN 0-7660-1243-3

CULTS
ISBN 0-89490-900-2

DEATH
An Introduction to Medical-Ethical Dilemmas
ISBN 0-7660-1246-8

DIVORCE
Young People Caught in the Middle
ISBN 0-89490-633-X

DRUG TESTING
An Issue for School, Sports, and Work
ISBN 0-89490-954-1

GAY AND LESBIAN RIGHTS
A Struggle
ISBN 0-89490-958-4

GUNS, VIOLENCE, AND TEENS
ISBN 0-89490-721-2

HATE GROUPS
Revised Edition
ISBN 0-7660-1245-X

THE HUNTING DEBATE
Aiming at the Issues
ISBN 0-7660-1110-0

THE INTERNET
Surfing the Issues
ISBN 0-89490-956-8

MILITIAS
Armed and Dangerous
ISBN 0-89490-902-9

NEO-NAZIS
A Growing Threat
ISBN 0-89490-901-0

PLAGUE AND PESTILENCE
A History of Infectious Disease
ISBN 0-89490-957-6

PORNOGRAPHY
Debating the Issues
ISBN 0-89490-907-X

PRISONS
Today's Debate
ISBN 0-89490-906-1

SCHOOL PRAYER
A History of Debate
ISBN 0-89490-904-5

SCHOOLS UNDER SIEGE
Guns, Gangs, and Hidden Dangers
ISBN 0-89490-908-8

SUICIDE
Tragic Choice
ISBN 0-7660-1105-4

TEEN RIGHTS
At Home, At School, Online
ISBN 0-7660-1242-5

TEEN SMOKING
Understanding the Risk
ISBN 0-89490-722-0

WOMEN IN COMBAT
The Battle for Equality
ISBN 0-7660-1103-8

Issues in Focus

Land Mines

100 Million Hidden Killers

Elaine Landau

Enslow Publishers, Inc.

40 Industrial Road
Box 398
Berkeley Heights, NJ 07922
USA

PO Box 38
Aldershot
Hants GU12 6BP
UK

http://www.enslow.com

Library of Congress Cataloging-in-Publication Data

Landau, Elaine.
Land mines: 100 million hidden killers/ Elaine Landau.
p. cm. – (Issues in focus)
Includes bibliographical references (p. 109) and index.
Summary: Describes dangers presented by land mines, their different types and uses, the fight to stop production, efforts to remove mines, attempts to regulate them, and help provided their victims.
ISBN 0-7660-1240-9 (hardcover)
1. Land mines—Juvenile literature. 2. Land mine victims—Juvenile literature. [1. Land mines.] I. Title. II. Series: Issues in focus (Hillside, N.J.).
UG490 .L36 2000
355.8'25115—dc21

99-050597
CIP

Printed in the United States of America

10 9 8 7 6 5 4 3 2 1

To Our Readers: All Internet addresses in this book were active and appropriate when we went to press. Any comments or suggestions can be sent by e-mail to Comments@enslow.com or to the address on the back cover.

Illustration Credits: American Red Cross, pp. 16, 18, 32, 46; Courtesy of Canadian Embassy, p. 93; Lutheran World Relief, pp. 11, 13, 79, 81; John Rodsted, pp. 20, 22; United Nations, p. 48; U.S. Army, pp. 52, 57, 59, 101; U.S. Department of Veteran Affairs, p. 75; U.S. Marine Corps, pp. 36, 41, 65; U.S. Navy, pp. 39, 55, 61; VVAF, p. 68.

Cover Illustration: © Robert Semeniuk.

Contents

1

Remnants of War

A ten-year-old girl delightedly skips across a field in Kosovo. She and her family have never been happier—they are on their way home. The family is among those who left their homeland during a bitter ethnic war. Clashes between ethnic Albanians and Serbian authorities had been going on for years. More recently, the Serbs had established a police state in Kosovo, terrorizing the ethnic Albanians and conducting an ethnic-cleansing campaign to reverse the area's ethnic and religious balance. The North Atlantic Treaty Organization (NATO, a confederation of sixteen Western nations which provides leadership for a unified offense) intervened, and by the summer of 1999 it was thought safe for civilians to return. But was it?

Less than a week after her return, the same young girl walked through another field much like the one she crossed on her way home. This time she never made it to the other side. A sudden explosion knocked her to the ground. Severely wounded, she was taken to a hospital where both her legs were amputated to save her life. The day before, she and her parents had discussed their hopes and dreams for her future. Now they wondered how they were going to pay for a wheelchair.

How her injury occurred after the war had ended was not a mystery. The girl stepped on a land mine left by soldiers. Both Serbian soldiers and members of the Kosovo Liberation Army relied heavily on land mines during the conflict. Humanitarian aid groups have tried to make the returning civilians aware of this problem.

Robert Coville, spokesperson for the United Nations High Commission for Refugees (UNHCR), has blanketed the region with leaflets and posters warning residents of the danger of undetonated mines that remained after the conflict. "We need to make these people understand that they must always be careful," he said. "It can be a hard message to get through."[1] The UNHCR and other agencies also launched a campaign warning farmers not to harvest the remains of this year's crops. Land mines, possibly buried in their fields, could mean the loss of a limb or a life.

"These people left a world they know very well and will return to an entirely different environment," noted Jessica Barry, spokesperson for the International Red Cross. "We need to make them understand that they'll have to live in a different way. They'll need to look at every patch of ground and consider whether it's been swept. They'll need to persuade curious children to resist picking up the most exotic objects they see."[2]

Among many of the adults, the message has already sunk in. "We will always be afraid now," said Kimete Adamah, a twenty-seven-year-old woman who fled after the Serbs started their ethnic-cleansing campaign. "Even though we are happy to go home, it will not be home like it was before. Now we will always wonder about what the children are playing with. You can be careful, but you can't watch them all the time."[3]

The Legacy of War—Hidden Killers

Unfortunately, the situation in Kosovo is not unique. Land mines are hidden killers that exist in many countries around the globe. One morning, Nhia Yeurung was awakened by a loud explosion outside his home in Cambodia near the Thailand border. Hearing his young grandson scream for help, he ran outside to find the small child lying in the road in a pool of blood. The little boy had stepped on a land mine.

The child's left leg was riddled with metal mine fragments and he was in a great deal of pain. As he knelt to pick up his grandson and stepped back to steady himself, Nhia Yeurung's right foot landed on another land mine. This time the older man and the child both nearly died in the blast.[4]

Those land mines had been left there by soldiers during a war that ended long ago. But that war is not over for civilians in the region, who are frequently killed or injured when they come into contact with one of the thousands of buried land mines.

Basilio, a young man from Angola, lost his right leg when he was just twelve years old. He had stepped on a land mine while playing soccer near his home. Due to his severe injuries, he had to leave school after the sixth grade. Before the accident Basilio dreamed of being an airline pilot or a soccer player. Today, he survives by cleaning shoes on his city's streets.[5]

Land Mine Statistics

The statistics on land mines are both frightening and sad. The U.S. Department of State has reported that land mines have been used in more than sixty countries by government and rebel movements. People are most affected by land mines in Afghanistan, Angola, Mozambique, Eritrea, Cambodia, Ethiopia, Iraq, Somalia, Sudan, and the former Yugoslavia.[6] Africa is the most heavily mined continent, with an estimated 20 million mines in eighteen countries.[7] According to UNICEF and other sources, there are more than 110 million land mines in existence today.[8]

Somewhere in the world, two thousand people

Luena, Angola, is ringed by minefields. People who step on land mines can lose one or both of their legs.

are involved in land mine accidents each month—a casualty every twenty minutes. Approximately eight hundred of these people die, and the rest are maimed.[9] Some humanitarian organizations believe the actual number of land mine casualties is much higher, but remains underreported because of the lack of emergency medical facilities and access to modern communication systems in some of the most heavily mined areas.

The use of land mines constitutes a war that continues even after the conflict they were intended for has ended. Land mines do not honor peace treaties or cease-fires. A land mine primed to explode cannot differentiate between a soldier's combat boot and the foot of a small child.

The International Campaign to Ban Land Mines (ICBL) is a coalition of one thousand nongovernmental organizations (NGOs) from more than fifty-five nations. In a report, ICBL stated: "After military conflicts end, all land mine casualties are civilian."[10] As a result, there are now two hundred fifty thousand amputees worldwide due to land mine injuries. U.S. Secretary of State Madeleine Albright noted that at the start of the twentieth century, 90 percent of wartime casualties were soldiers, while at the close of this century, 90 percent are civilians.[11] Unfortunately, that continues to be the case.

The Risks for Children

Children are among the most at risk of being killed or maimed by land mines. That is partly because they

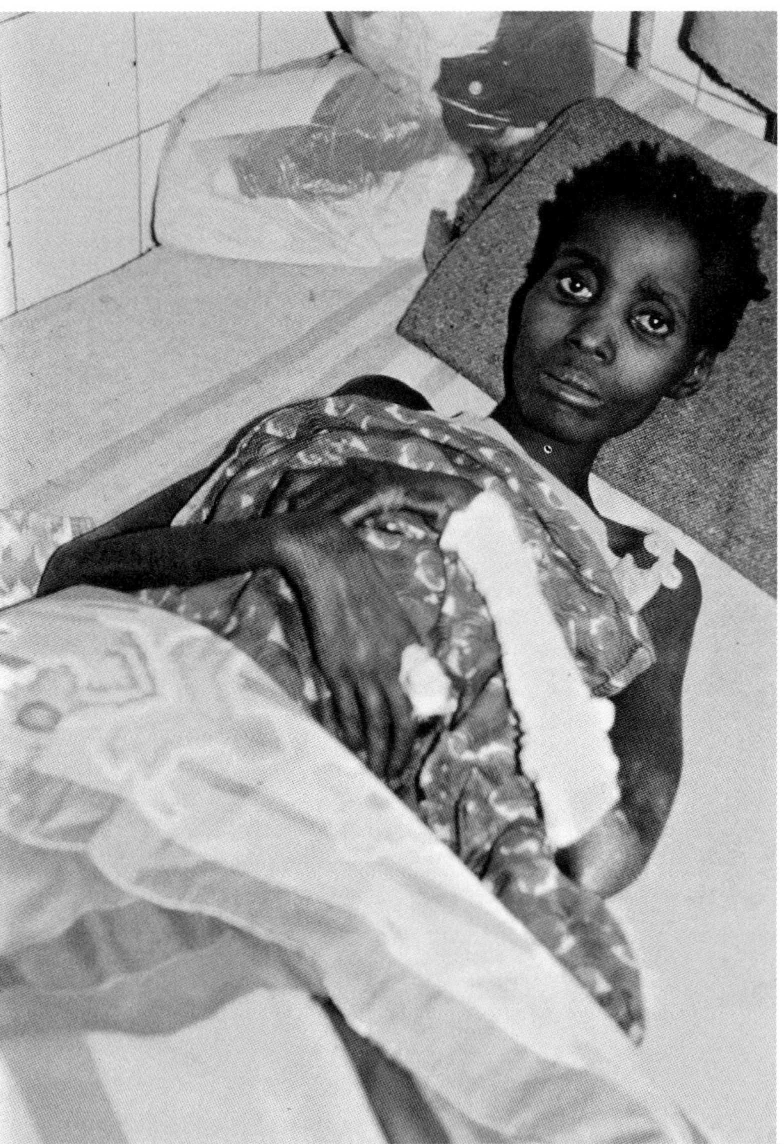

Maria Jamba needed to feed her children. She went into the bush to get firewood to sell and stepped on a land mine. By the time she was brought to the hospital, gangrene had set in.

are often not fully aware of the dangers of land mines as they walk to school, do chores, or play outdoors. At times, just being small makes children especially vulnerable. Rae McGrath, director of the Mines Advisory Group, explained how this is so:

> I was examining the site of a mine incident in northern Iraq/Kurdistan where a six-year-old boy had died. The boy had strayed into a minefield while playing, but it was not clear at all how he could have possibly stood on a mine accidentally; the mines, all surfacelaid pressure devices, were clearly visible, and it was unlikely that a boy from a village in a heavily mined area would not have recognized them as mines. The area was grassland meadow, and it was only when I crouched to inspect the accident site that I suddenly realized why the boy had died. Although the grass was no more than six inches high, from my new position I could see no mines: I could only see grass. My eye level was roughly that of a boy of six. The victim died because he was too small.[12]

Children often mistake the small, colorful plastic land mines for toys. Le Van Nahn of Vietnam was playing with his friends when the boys found a small land mine that looked like a toy. He recalled:

> I was eleven years old when the accident happened on the way to school with some friends. We saw the [land mine]; it was round and small like an orange. We had no idea what it was. Huv [his friend] picked it up from the side of the road, and we played with it like it was a small piece of fruit.
>
> We wanted to see who could throw it further. It exploded when Huv threw it. I did not know what

> happened. Seeing my friends lying on the ground and a lot of blood frightened me. . . . I remember someone running from the village and picking me up. . . . After I came home from the hospital I was unable to move on my own, so I stayed inside. If I wanted to go anywhere, my brother had to carry me on his back. I couldn't go to school because I had no way to get there.[13]

In November 1993, six-year-old Sia Ya and her four-year-old brother Kou Ya of Laos were leading a water buffalo to pasture when they noticed a round object in a ditch. They thought it was a ball like the ones boys and girls toss during Hmong New Year festivities, but it was actually a land mine. Sia Ya threw the mine to her little brother. It exploded, killing both children and severely wounding a passing cyclist.[14]

Physicians for Human Rights, a humanitarian organization founded in 1986, has sent over forty teams of physicians and scientists to thirty-five countries to aid those in need of urgent medical care. In February 1992, two doctors from Physicians for Human Rights were at a hospital in northern Somalia when they examined a six-year-old land mine victim. The boy had picked up a small antipersonnel land mine near his house. He had mistaken it for a thermos bottle top. The explosion blinded the boy and badly scarred his face and knees. His right hand also had to be amputated.[15] Those fortunate enough to survive a land mine explosion are usually severely wounded. Rae McGrath and Eric Stover noted in their article, "Injuries From Land Mines," which appeared in the *British Medical Journal*:

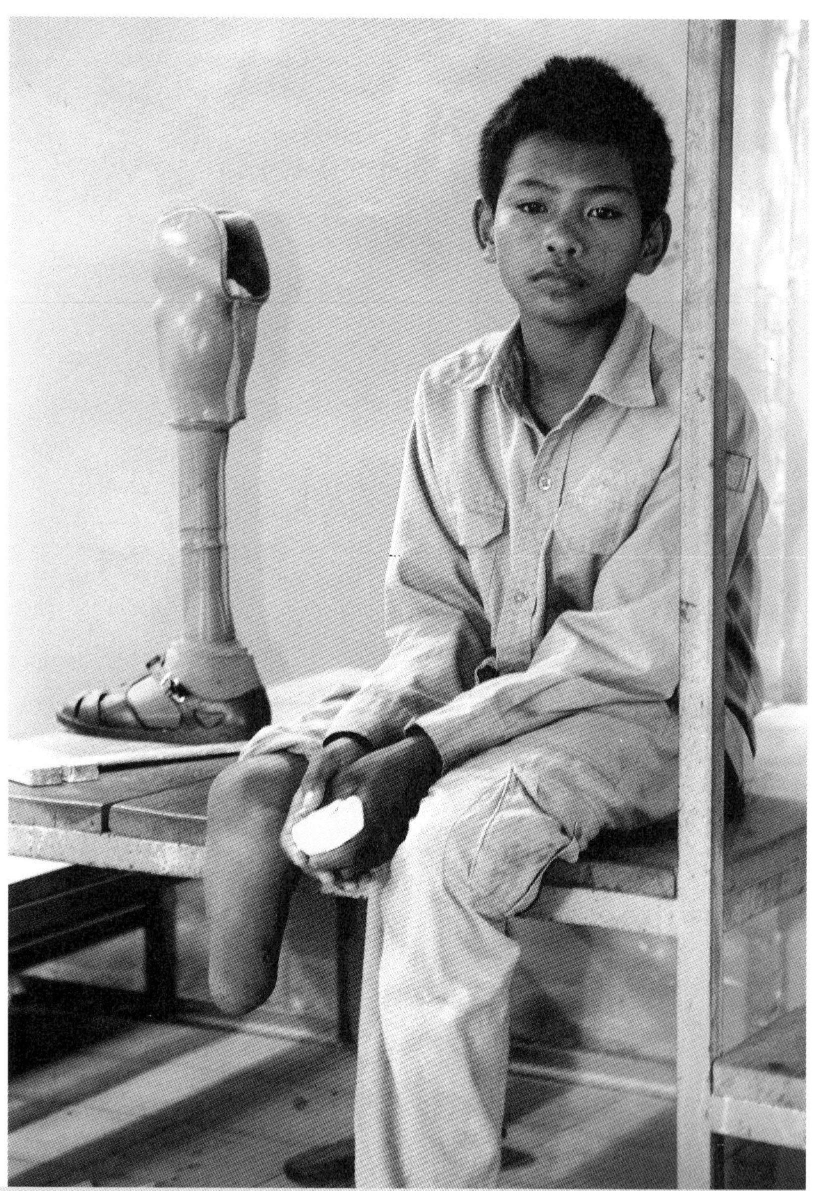

Children sometimes pick up land mines because they are brightly colored, and look like toys or even bottle tops.

> Land mines . . . have ruinous effects on the human body: they drive dirt, bacteria, clothing, and metal and plastic into the tissue, causing secondary infections. The shock wave from an exploding mine can destroy blood vessels well up the leg, causing surgeons to amputate much higher than the site of the primary wound.[16]

Many doctors who work with land mine victims find their patients' injuries especially hard to deal with. "You have to accept amputations as the only way to help people. And you have to find ways to evacuate your feelings when you're doing it," explained Swiss surgeon Bernard Vermuelen. Yet his patients' wounds continued to upset him—especially those of a boy about his son's age who had to have both his legs amputated. "He [the child] was not at war," Vermuelen noted, "but the victim of a weapon used to terrorize civilians."[17]

The terror is ongoing. It is an inescapable reality for the millions of people around the world who live in land-mine-infested nations. Vermont Senator Patrick Leahy aptly summed up their predicament when he told Congress,

> Think of the horror of living day to day in a country where at any moment you could lose a leg, or your life, or your child's life, because of these hidden weapons. Where any open field, or patch of trees, or roadside ditch is a potential death trap. That is a way of life for tens of millions of people around the world.[18]

The Danger of Daily Tasks

The existence of these weapons turns daily tasks such as collecting firewood, fetching water, putting

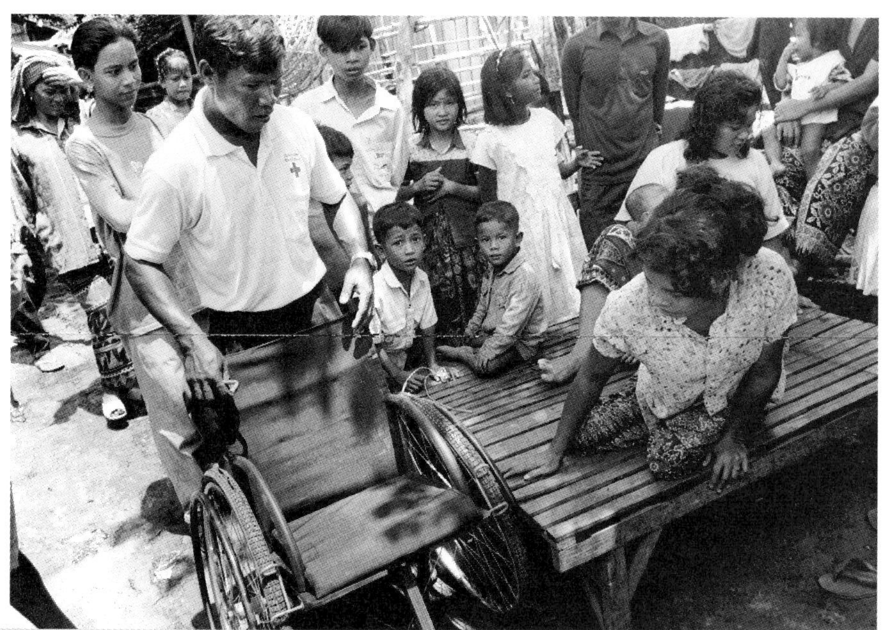

Sometimes land mine damage is so severe that a child will lose both legs and only be able to get around in a wheelchair—a very expensive item, especially in a poor country.

animals out to graze, and planting or harvesting crops into high-risk, potentially devastating activities. In August 1993, Nang Saiko, a widow from Laos, was working in the garden with her daughter Posua, when the girl's hoe struck a land mine. The blast killed Posua and severely wounded Nang Saiko in the leg. Flying shrapnel also hit Nang Saiko's younger daughter in the face. "Unfortunately," explained an official from the province's Public Social Welfare Department, "Nang Saiko's situation is not uncommon. Every village in this area has stories like that."[19] Although Nang Saiko has little food to feed her five surviving children, she is now afraid to tend her rice field.

In another part of Laos, a man lit a fire close to his home to boil water for morning tea. At the time, he had no way of knowing that a land mine was buried in the ground. Yet, as the fire warmed the earth, it triggered the mine, which exploded. The pot and the ground around it shot through the air, narrowly missing the man, who stood nearby. The women in the area now say that they no longer build their cooking fires on new spots.[20]

Lack of Prompt Medical Care

Just because a person has been hurt in a land mine explosion does not mean that he or she will always receive speedy or competent medical attention. Sadly, in developing countries, sometimes half of those involved in land mine accidents die because they are unable to get the necessary medical care. It

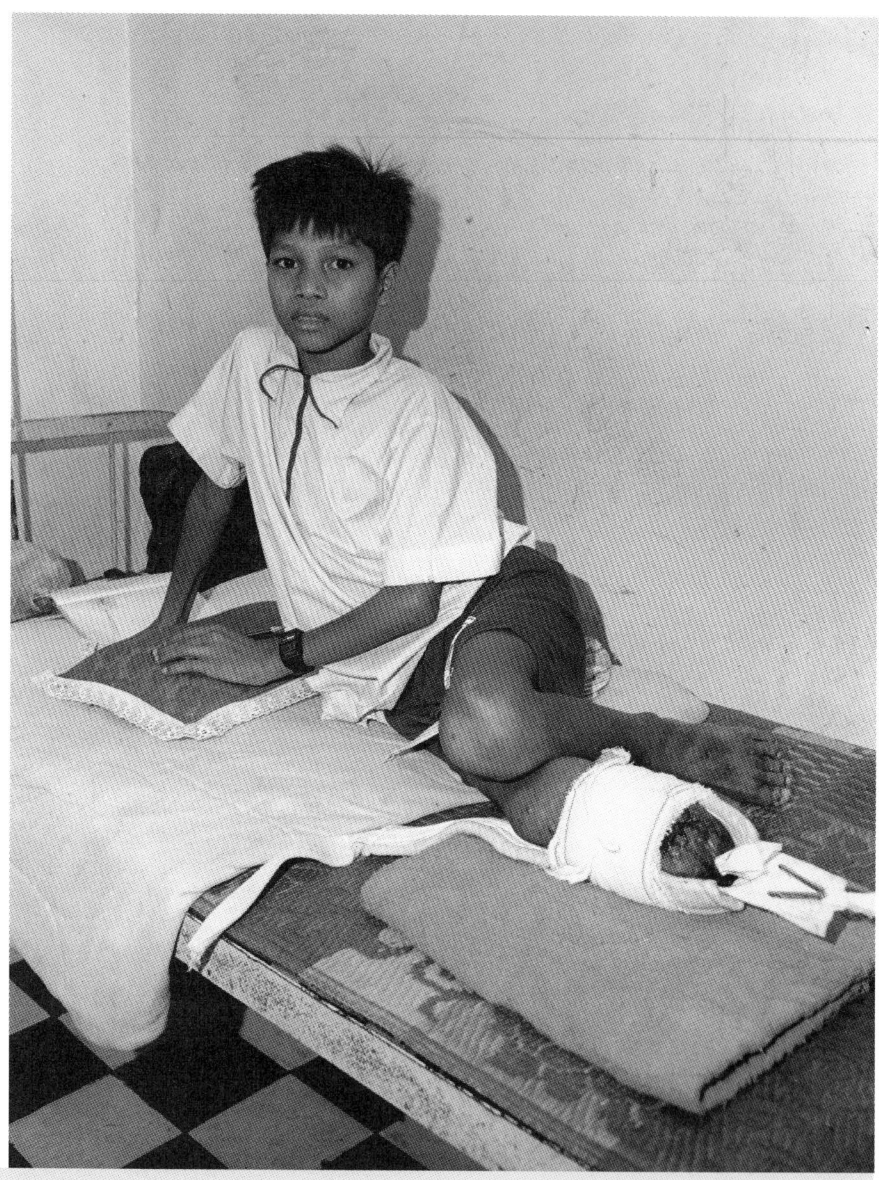

Children are among the most at risk from land mine accidents.

is estimated that in Cambodia, for example, for every person who gets to a hospital, another dies in the fields.[21]

An individual who survives the blast will need a bystander willing to risk carrying him or her out of the mined vicinity. This is often a dangerous task because there might be other land mines nearby that could go off. Also, the rescuer has to find others willing to take the injured individual to the nearest emergency medical center. These people may want to be paid, and if the injured person does not have the money, the search for assistance may be over. Or, on the other hand, if a hospital or other medical facility cannot be reached, medical intervention will also become impossible.

The luckiest land mine survivors get help, as did nine-year-old Fernando Moises, who in 1995 stepped on a land mine while looking for firewood near his home in Angola. The explosion blew the boy's leg off. Unable to move, he clung to life while lying on the ground for nearly two hours until he was found by some neighbors. They carried Fernando on foot to the nearest hospital, which was about four miles (seven kilometers) away. There, the doctors miraculously managed to save his life.[22]

Elizete Manhica of Mozambique was not so fortunate. On the morning of March 13, 1996, she awoke early, as usual, to tend her small farm in Maputo, the country's capital. While gathering dry grass, Elizete felt something strange in the ground. She took a hoe and beat the land to remove the object. Suddenly, the object exploded, blowing her

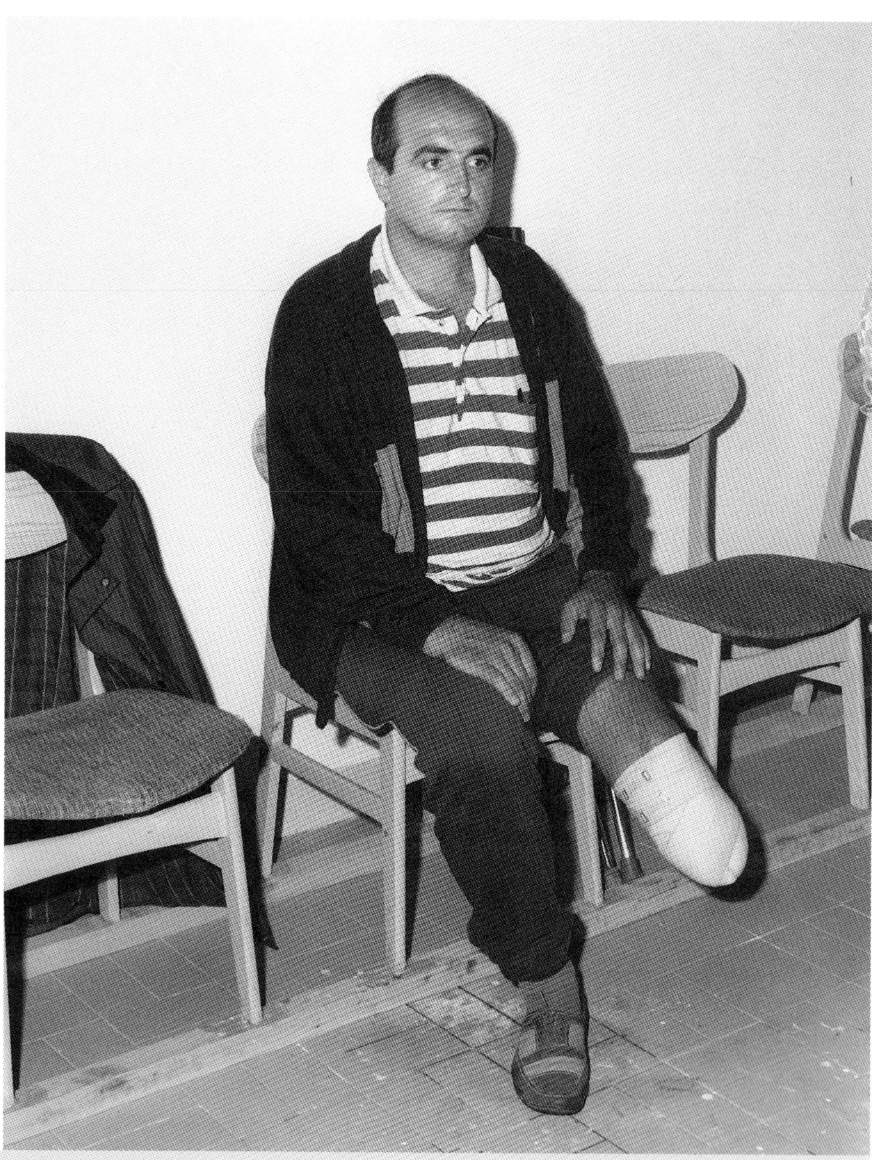

Worldwide, two thousand people are involved in land mine accidents each month—a casualty every twenty minutes.

body back a distance. She tried to get up but was unable to do so. Help came after some friends nearby heard the explosion and Elizete's screams for assistance. But it was too late. Elizete died on the way to the hospital. She was not the only one who suffered as a result of the land mine explosion. Her three children are now orphans because their father died during the war in which the land mines were laid.[23]

Civilians without access to rapid transport have frequently died en route to hospitals because of extensive blood loss. A study of Cambodian land mine survivors done by Physicians for Human Rights and Asia Watch found "that for mine-blast victims from rural areas, an average of twelve hours elapsed from the moment of injury until they reached a hospital with surgical facilities."[24]

Another study indicated that out of 757 land mine injury patients treated in hospitals in developing countries, most arrived there between six and fourteen hours after the injury occurred.[25]

Lack of Treatment for the Poor

Even if a land mine survivor is able to get to a medical facility, he or she will frequently have to pay for the medical services. "Once survivors of land mine injuries reach a . . . hospital, they find that there is little or no food except what relatives bring," an observer from Physicians for Human Rights noted.

> Mine blast patients often have to pay physicians and nurses for their services, medicine, and intravenous fluids. If blood is needed the patient's family may have to find donors and pay them.

> Patients with mine blast injuries often require twice as much blood as patients wounded by other munitions.[26]

One Cambodian woman whose son stepped on a land mine while tending their cow described her experience at the hospital:

> In the hospital at Battambang, they didn't give away a single tablet. We had to pay for everything. When we first got there, I had no money. . . . We just waited. . . . He [her son] was screaming with pain and would shout, "Mother, I want some water." . . . I said to the doctor, "Please take pity on my son, he's desperate for a drink and he's so badly injured." The doctor said, "Have you any money?"

When the woman told him she didn't, he walked away. About a half hour later the same doctor came back and said, "If you don't have any money how can we amputate his leg? He'll need some blood transfusions and some other medicines."[27]

Fortunately, the woman was with her uncle, who immediately went to the local pawnbroker to pawn what little they had. He came back with enough cash to buy serum, medication, and most importantly, to pay for the surgery. All the while, the woman had waited at the hospital, still holding her injured child. Although her uncle had returned by 5 P.M., her son had not yet been treated at 10 P.M., while others with more money were treated immediately.

At about midnight, the boy was finally operated on. Unable to afford nursing care, the family took turns looking after the child through the night. In the morning, the hospital janitor handed the distraught mother her son's bloody clothes and the amputated portion of his leg and told her to go bury them. She explained that she could not leave the building because she still had her younger children with her to care for. In the end, she had to pay the janitor to dispose of these items for her.

In some very poor countries, these fees discourage people from even attempting to get help. This is especially true in some places if the person is very badly hurt, elderly or female, and therefore considered less valuable in that culture. Even those who get help sometimes lose a limb that might have been saved because the tourniquet used to stop the bleeding was left on too long. In other instances, transportation delays in remote areas cause the patient to arrive at the hospital too late to save the limb. At times, countries lack adequate medical supplies, such as antibiotics and intravenous fluids, which hinders the medical team's chances of saving a patient's arm or leg.

Often there are also few government programs to provide necessary care after patients leave the hospital. Most land mine amputees leave hospitals without referrals to be fitted for artificial limbs, which would help them to resume a more normal life. Young children frequently fare the worst; they are most in need of follow-up care because the bone of the amputation stump in a young person grows faster than the surrounding skin and tissue. The child may need additional surgery to prevent infection, sores, and pain. The surgeries may also be necessary for an artificial limb to fit properly.

Yet, even when artificial limbs are available, they are often out of the financial reach of land mine survivors. According to the International Committee of the Red Cross, "a prosthesis [artificial limb] for a child should be replaced every six months, and for an adult every three to five years. A ten-year-old with a life expectancy of another forty or fifty years will need twenty-five prostheses, at a total cost of $3,125 in his or her lifetime."[28]

Isolation and Exile

In some parts of the world, land mine survivors who lose limbs also lose far more. An article in *Business News* described the life of an amputee in Cambodia as "worse than dying":

> Cambodians believe that a person missing a limb is not whole. A body missing a part means the spirit is incomplete. So the maimed are shunned. No one hires them. And if there are no family members who will support them, they must beg for food. Many commit suicide or spend their lives shut away, afraid to venture out.[29]

Besides the physical harm and societal isolation they cause, land mines also make resettlement extremely difficult for civilians hoping to return home after a conflict. People and communities need land to sustain their lives and cultures. Yet these killing devices ensure that large tracts of rural farmland remain unusable for raising farm animals or growing crops. Land mines disrupt access to water and grazing land. These weapons also pose a threat to a country's wildlife, which discourages the tourism that can bring financial resources to many developing nations. Tourists want to be able to see wildlife without risking their lives and limbs.

Since jeeps, trucks, and other vehicles cannot travel safely through villages and fields where there are land mines, transportation and supply routes are often blocked in these areas, and medical and educational services cannot be established for local residents. In the worst cases, this can lead to starvation and famine. Current figures indicate that between 13 million and 18 million people worldwide die of starvation annually, or about seventeen hundred individuals a day. Although it is difficult to determine precisely how many of these deaths are directly connected to land mines, their presence can severely hurt a community's ability to find food.

Such situations can also increase the flow of refugees with nowhere to go, as large numbers of people are either forced to leave or unable to return to their country or village after a conflict. Normal movement and job possibilities become sharply limited. A recent report from the United Nations High Commission for Refugees forecast that ". . . although the number of people forced to abandon their homes across the world continues to rise, fewer will be able to find safe refuge."[30] The document stated that by the start of 1997, approximately 22.7 million people were at risk, over half from such heavily mined countries as Afghanistan, Angola, Bosnia, Cambodia,

Croatia, Eritrea, Iraq, Mozambique, Somalia, and Sudan.

In less time than it takes to read this book, somewhere in the world, someone is dying or suffering because of a land mine. That is a high price to pay for a killing device that might not even be essential in military operations. One study endorsed by high-ranking military officers from a number of countries found that in none of the twenty-six conflicts since 1940 where land mines were used did land mines play a major role in determining the outcome.

2

The Killing Fields

Land mines are equal-opportunity weapons. Anyone, regardless of age, race, or origin can be killed or maimed by them. But while all land mine explosions have a similar result, there are many types of mines. Antitank and antipersonnel land mines have both been used extensively. Antipersonnel (AP) mines are designed to hurt people rather than to destroy army tanks or other military vehicles. These mines are encased explosive devices that are usually buried beneath the ground, or, in some instances, placed on or near the ground. The various types of antipersonnel mines may be set off by a person, a timing device, or remote control.

More than three hundred fifty different kinds of antipersonnel mines exist. They are manufactured in more than fifty countries in various parts of the world. The following are the major types of antipersonnel mines.

Blast Mines

Blast mines are the most common type of antipersonnel land mine used worldwide. Planted in the ground like deadly seeds, they are impossible for passersby to detect. If stepped on, they go off with a deadly explosive force designed to rip apart flesh and bone. The PMN (personnel mine nonmetallic), which has an especially large explosive charge, is among the blast mines credited with having killed more civilians than most other types of blast mines. Even if found and dug up, it is almost impossible to make sure these mines are no longer harmful. The PMN is largely manufactured in the former Soviet Union and Iraq.

Fragmentation Mines

These mines are activated by difficult-to-see trip wires lying just fractions of an inch above the ground. When activated, fragmentation mines shoot out hundreds of sharp metal fragments at twice the speed of a standard bullet, killing people within a thirteen-foot radius. Such mines are sometimes called stake mines, because they may also be mounted on stakes or tied to trees in places where the underbrush hides them. Some types of fragmentation mines are planted in clusters for greater impact.

The POMZ-2 (antipersonnel fragmentation obstacle mine) is a stake or fragmentation mine. Largely manufactured in the former Soviet Union, it was extensively used in Cambodia. When a person steps on a POMZ-2's trip wire, the pressure pulls the pin from the top of the fuse. Its removal causes a spring-loaded needle to strike the percussion cap, which makes the mine explode. The expanding gases produced by the explosion propel the pieces of the mine's shattered iron casings through the air with dynamic force.

Bounding Fragmentation Mines

Bounding fragmentation mines combine the worst aspects of fragmentation mines with horrible features of their own. When activated, a bounding fragmentation mine flies up to about the height of an adult's chest before exploding into fragments. In some types, more than one thousand metal fragments will shoot out over a radius of twenty to thirty meters (sixty to one hundred feet). This generally means that someone who activates one of these mines will be killed. The shooting fragments also kill or wound more people over a broader area than a similarly sized mine that explodes on or in the ground.

Among the most widely deployed bounding fragmentation mines is the Type 69, made in China and in a number of other countries as well. Also known

Once a person has been wounded by a land mine, the ground never feels safe to walk on again.

as a "Bounding Betty," the Type 69 has a plastic case with a removable fuse mounted on top. This mine can be set off either by trip wires connected to its fuse prongs or by stepping on it. This type of mine is usually well-camouflaged. When exploded, the mine scatters about two hundred forty fragments over an eleven-meter (thirty-eight-foot) radius.

Directional Fragmentation Mines

Filled with steel pellets on one side of an explosive charge, this type of mine shoots out hard balls at high speeds in a specific direction. Such land mines can be set off by trip wires or even by remote control. Some varieties can kill from as far away as 656 feet.

Scatterable Mines

Unlike mines which have to be planted in the ground, scatterable mines are laborsaving killing devices. Large numbers of these mines can be scattered about by airplanes or even artillery. Such mines are designed to land on the ground without exploding, and some can even lay out their own trip wires.

An early type of blast mine is shaped like a butterfly and glides to the ground. Some of these plastic mines are small enough to fit in the palm of your hand and will explode if handled or stepped on. They are painted green and tan to readily blend in with the surroundings. Regrettably, these qualities also make them especially appealing to children, who tend to pick them up thinking they are toys.

Smart Mines

"Smart" or "self-destruct" mines are technologically advanced land mines. These new mines are designed to blow themselves up after a set number of weeks or months, or to "self-deactivate" (stop working) once their batteries run out. Some military experts believe that they are a safe alternative to traditional land mines. But it has been estimated that 20 to 30 percent of these mines will fail to either self-destruct or self-deactivate. And Kathryn Wolford, president of Lutheran World Relief, a New York-based international relief and development organization, stated ". . . no matter how 'smart' it is, the mine would not be able to distinguish between a military vehicle and a donkey cart."[1]

Antitank Mines

Unlike antipersonnel land mines, antitank (AT) mines were intended to blow up military tanks or heavy vehicles. According to the United Nations Department of Humanitarian Affairs, antitank mines contain higher levels of explosives than antipersonnel mines and are designed to be triggered by vehicles, but cannot distinguish among tanks, tractors, or relief trucks. When an antitank mine explodes, it usually kills occupants of light vehicles.

Mines like the Russian TM-57 can contain as much as seven grams of the high explosive TNT within their green steel casings. Although these potent devices were built to demolish large weapons, they have sometimes been used in areas where war was mostly waged on foot. At times, they were planted to frighten the enemy by delivering a blast sufficiently powerful to kill a large number of foot soldiers. In some areas, whole stacks of antitank mines have been found lying on top of 120-millimeter mortar shells. There is no reason why they should have been left that way, but some people think that since these mines are heavy, soldiers, tired of carrying them, decided to drop them all at once.

Land Mines Sown in Civilian Settlements

Presently, people in many parts of the world are struggling to deal with the effects of both antitank and antipersonnel land mines planted in areas that were never really battle sites. In some cases, troops deliberately planted them near civilian settlements to strategically control the comings and goings of enemy populations and insure that villagers did not assist the enemy.

In numerous instances, many thousands of land mines were planted near hamlets, cities, railways, airports, farms, bridges, and well-used footpaths. Often they were placed beneath downed trees to block roads permanently. In one case in Angola, a local army officer circled his farm with land mines to prevent hungry villagers from stealing fruits and vegetables from his garden. At great expense to those who ventured near, "his neatly terraced garden [was] the greenest in Luena," noted author Philip C. Winslow in his book *Sowing the Dragon's Teeth: Land Mines and the Global Legacy of War.*[2]

At Camp Lejuene, North Carolina, two marines hold mines used for training during a field exercise.

Haphazard Placement

Ideally, any army would place both its antipersonnel and antitank explosive devices methodically and carefully. Army manuals from numerous nations recommend keeping accurate maps and records of all land mine placement. That would certainly lessen safety concerns and make postwar demining efforts more efficient. Yet, more often than not, it does not happen that way. Land mines are frequently laid haphazardly, with little thought given to consequences. In countries where conflicts have gone on continuously for a number of years, many of the soldiers who might have been able to say where the mines were have been killed. In some instances, soldiers have even fallen victims to land mines they planted earlier. One infantryman recalled how this can happen:

> On my first active duty we had a leader who kept a notebook about where we put mines. All the experienced fighters laughed at that and asked, "Who will read such a book?" I thought it was a good idea but only if others did the same thing and, of course, they don't. Last year we were ordered to put mines near a path. As we were doing this, I had a feeling—you know—when you think you know a place, that you have been in that place before. Anyway, my attention was distracted because one of the others [a soldier] was blown up, then the man on my right shouted that we were in a minefield and started to walk back to the path and he stood on a mine. . . . I knew then why I knew the place. . . . I had put mines there only three months before.[3]

Long, Destructive History

Land mines are not new weapons. This type of warfare actually dates back to the Renaissance. Warring factions dug tunnels near an enemy's castle and packed them with gunpowder. The idea was to incapacitate the opponent's army when it left the fortress. In the United States, mines were first used by both sides during the Civil War. Yet when an oversized mine killed and maimed a large number of Confederate and Union soldiers as well as some civilians at the siege of Petersburg, Virginia, even Union General William Tecumseh Sherman referred to such devices as "a violation of civilized warfare."

Nevertheless, land mines continued to be used and improved upon in wars. These weapons truly came of age in World War I. The Germans tried to destroy French and British tanks by burying artillery shells along established vehicle routes. When in the 1920s the powerful lightweight explosive TNT was invented, engineers were able to create more precise and dependable antitank mines, which later became popular weapons in World War II. The antitank mines used in World War II were flat, steel cylinders less than two feet in diameter that were filled with about twenty-five pounds of TNT. While both sides had mines, Germany and the Soviet Union used them most extensively. It has been estimated that more than 222 million land mines were planted during this war by the Soviet Union's army alone.

Two members of an explosive ordnance disposal team work together to mark the location of possible mines found with the aid of a metal detector on the beach.

Growing Sophistication

Before long, however, combatants realized that these large antitank mines could be readily found by the enemy's mine detectors and subsequently dug up and used to their opponent's advantage. To stop this practice, the first antipersonnel mines were developed and buried near the larger antitank mines. The small antipersonnel mines usually consisted of a metal or glass container holding less than a pound of explosive—just enough to kill or maim a soldier. These smaller mines were much harder to detect, and made digging up antitank mines extremely dangerous.

During the 1950s and 1960s, more sophisticated land mines were created. In the 1960s, the United States dropped scatterable land mines from airplanes in Southeast Asia. The main purpose of these mines was to maim rather than kill. The idea was to slow the enemy's troop movements by forcing them to deal with numerous casualties along the way. Military experts hoped the injured soldiers' screams would intimidate and demoralize others in their squad. In addition, the vehicles and helicopters brought in to evacuate the wounded were likely to add to the commotion and further stop enemy soldiers from doing what they set out to do.

Land mine manufacturers began to gear their products toward this goal. One sales brochure from a Pakistani land mine company emphasized that the small amount of explosive in their new land mines would "make the man disabled and incapacitate him

Bounding mines are displayed during a Marine training exercise in Camp Lejuene, North Carolina.

permanently" because "operating research has shown that it is better to disable the enemy than kill him."[4] As a result, so many scatterable land mines were dropped from airplanes over Vietnam that the pilots nicknamed these weapons "garbage."

Throughout the conflict in Vietnam, other types of land mines were extensively used by both sides as well. In 1965, land mines and booby traps were responsible for nearly 70 percent of United States Marine casualties. A Pentagon study following the war indicated that between one-fifth and one-third of all American deaths in Vietnam (from ten thousand to eighteen thousand people) resulted from land mines.

In the years since, land mines have been increasingly used by various nations throughout the world. Often they are employed offensively to direct enemy troops into ambushes or make entire villages unsafe for refuge by the enemy. Since antipersonnel mines are light and inexpensive, they became a favorite weapon in civil wars and rebel uprisings in many places. The United States Defense Agency summed up the increasing popularity of land mines in a 1992 report:

> Even with relatively costly new technologies, land mines are an affordable weapon for the entire range of military organizations from terrorist groups to large, well-equipped armies and will continue to be a significant element in armed conflicts at all levels of intensity well into the foreseeable future.[5]

For these reasons, the use of land mines is

increasing. Physicians Against Land Mines (PALM), a humanitarian anti–land mine group, estimates that for every one hundred thousand mines removed, another 1 million to 2 million new ones are planted.[6] These are used in both new and ongoing conflicts. The cost of planting land mines is relatively low. The postwar cost to civilians remains immeasurable.

3

The Comings and Goings of Land Mines

The increasing use of land mines has provided numerous arms companies with great profits. A large number of the world's arms producers manufacture and export land mines or parts used for land mines. This occurs in countries that include China, the former Soviet Union, India, Pakistan, Italy, South Africa, the United States, and the Federal Republic of Yugoslavia (FRY). FRY was established after the breakup of the former Yugoslavia and consists of two republics, Serbia and Montenegro.

Human-rights groups have frequently found it difficult to obtain accurate information on land mine production. Recent negative publicity has made many companies reluctant to release data on land mine production. In various parts of the world where these weapons are manufactured by government-owned businesses, production information is often not made public.

Monitoring Production and Sales

The Arms Project division of Human Rights Watch was formed in 1992 to monitor arms transfers to governments or organizations that grossly violate human rights or the laws of war. It identified nearly one hundred businesses (some government-owned) in numerous nations that have recently produced hundreds of different types of land mines. China, Italy, and the former Soviet Union were found to be the largest land mine producers and exporters.

Human Rights Watch also surveyed all of the United States companies producing land mines. Before publishing the study's results, the organization contacted the manufacturers and informed them of the vast civilian casualties caused by land mines, and urged them to stop making these weapons. Of the forty-seven United States weapons manufacturing companies that produce land mines, seventeen, including Motorola, which took the lead, publicly agreed to halt production.

No More "Business as Usual"

Perhaps the most dramatic change of policy from a land mine producer did not involve a United States

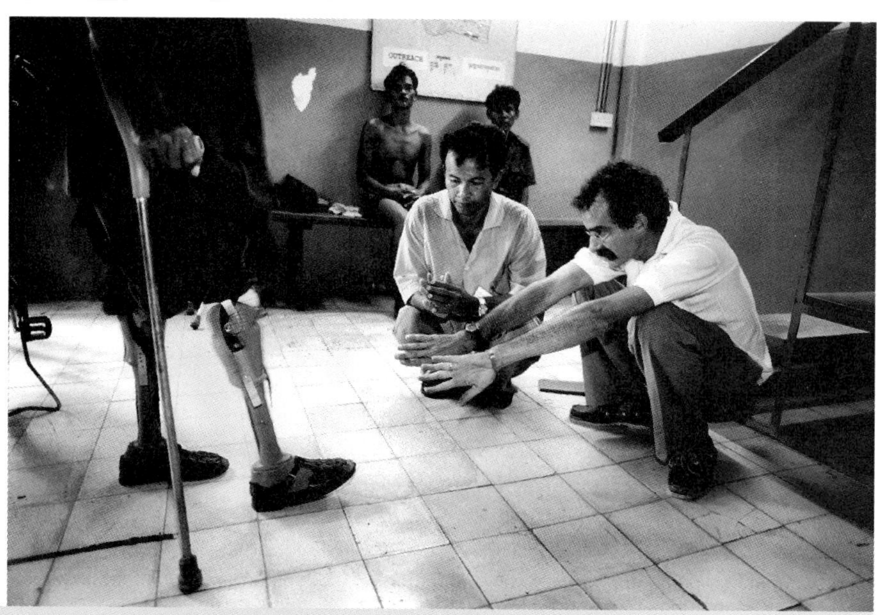

It takes time and can be extremely difficult to learn to walk with both a prosthesis and a cane after losing one's legs.

corporation, but instead came from Vito Alfiere Fontana's family-owned Technover company in Italy. Technover was one of Italy's largest producers of antipersonnel land mines. Fontana, trained as an electrical engineer, had worked in many aspects of land mine production, including sales. Yet, after seeing the civilian mine casualties firsthand, he could no longer do business as usual.

"I talked with Italian deminers working in Bosnia and later with Kurdish army officers," Fontana recalled. "The deminers told me of the horrible use and consequences of mines in Bosnia, and a Kurdish officer told me, 'Children are dying. We must stop this altogether.' I struggled with my conscience but soon realized that a total ban was the only answer."[1]

In 1993, Technover stopped producing land mines. Since then, Fontana has assisted nongovernmental organizations such as Human Rights Watch to identify companies involved in making mines and mine components. "What mines are doing around the world is appalling, and we must assume much responsibility for making them so easy to use and so available," Fontana said.[2]

Many Nations Continue to Produce Land Mines

But the fight is far from over for human-rights groups hoping to stop land mine production in the United States. Seventeen companies in the Human Rights Watch study refused to change their production plans, while another thirteen failed to respond to the

Croatian and Serbian deminers worked together to clear thousands of land mines from civilian areas damaged by war.

survey. Following the study, Human Rights Watch continued to exert pressure on the land mine–producing concerns. At first, representatives of some companies expressed surprise at being named in the survey, while others adamantly denied participating in the land mine business. Even after Human Rights Watch sent them irrefutable evidence, such as copies of invoices from the Defense Department, some companies continued to deny their involvement. Human Rights Watch could not make them admit their involvement. The group has the power to expose, but not to punish.

Monitoring Remains Essential

Nevertheless, monitoring land mine manufacturing is essential, since the Arms Project of Human Rights Watch stresses that "land mine production is a changing, growing business." According to the Project: "In some countries and for some companies, land mine production is assuming increased economic importance as part of the move toward increasingly sophisticated ground warfare technology. Moreover, producers are pursuing potentially profitable new markets for both scatterable mine systems and for more sophisticated variants of the conventional AP land mine."[3]

Removing Land Mines

In addition to concerns about the manufacture and use of land mines, there is also the monumental problem of demining, or removing land mines from the ground. Demining, anywhere in the world, is a difficult and dangerous task. As noted earlier, it is estimated that there are about 110 million land mines scattered in more than 70 nations.[4] In other words, for every seventeen children or fifty-two adults in the world, a land mine is planted somewhere. Besides the land mines waiting to be detonated, another 110 million have been stockpiled.[5]

Although approximately one hundred thousand mines are removed annually, until fairly recently an additional 1 to 2 million were planted each year. That means that new mines are being placed at a rate of ten or more times faster than deminers are removing them. At the present rate of demining, it would take 1,100 years to have a world free of mines, assuming that no additional mines are laid. The Arms Project of Human Rights Watch says that the world will probably never be totally rid of all the land mines planted. "Large parts of the world will never be demined," the group predicts. "Some areas mined during World War II have never been properly cleared, even after fifty years. . . . In countries like Afghanistan and Cambodia, the mine infestations are so large that there is no hope of clearing them all. . . . In Cambodia, it is likely that many of the large border minefields will be marked but not cleared, leaving thousands of mines in place. . . . In areas that are cleared, it is not realistic to expect that each and every mine will be removed and destroyed."[6]

The Expense of Removing Land Mines

Land mine removal is extremely expensive. Land mines only cost from three to thirty dollars to buy, but removing one can cost about fifty times that much. Unfortunately, getting land mines out of the ground remains a slow, high-risk, labor-intensive process. It takes days just to clear a small area. This is especially true of places where mines were planted more than twenty years ago and are now covered by a thick undergrowth.

Since World War II, more advances have been achieved in developing and placing mines than in mine clearance. The newer antipersonnel land mines are smaller and more cheaply made, with so little metal that they are often missed by standard mine detectors. And while the cost of the time-consuming and extremely dangerous process of manually removing mines remains high, there is not enough money to complete the work. In 1996, the United Nations secretary general increased his estimate of the funds needed to clear all existing mines from $33 billion to over $50 billion—but unfortunately, the funding allotted for demining was under $150 million.[7] This does not include the additional demining costs that come with injury, medical care, or impassable roads.

The Need for New Technology

The situation desperately calls for new technology and techniques in mine clearance. For now, crude metal detectors are used to determine suspected land mine territory inch by inch. As Ambassador Karl

Two soldiers use mine detectors fitted with microcomputer circuitry to locate land mines. The new circuitry gives the detectors improved performance in desert soils.

Inderfurth, United States Special Representative to the President and Secretary of State for Global Humanitarian Demining, said in December 1997, "We need to intensify research into better methods of demining . . . the most common tool we have for detecting land mines is still a [metal detector on a] stick attached to a person's arm."[8]

As Inderfurth indicated, in many countries people clear land mines with the same tools they used more than fifty years ago at the end of World War II. That is often because huge, heavy demining equipment such as armor-plated plows are of no use in a forest or rice paddy. This means that most mine clearance continues to be done by teams of individual deminers scanning the ground with metal detectors. Once a mine has been identified, the deminer gets down on his or her hands and knees wearing a special face guard and probes the earth inch by inch to find the telltale metal. He or she then meticulously clears away the dust with a small brush until the mine is unearthed.

Sensitive instruments called mine detectors locate mines that have metal, rather than plastic, cases. The fastest way to detect a mine is by mounting a mine-detecting device on a jeep. However, using a vehicle makes the procedure more expensive.

The experience of Francisco Muiengo, a deminer in Angola, is typical of others doing the same task around the world:

> Francisco Muiengo keeps sweeping his detector over one spot and getting the same signal. The Ebinger detector . . . tells the young mine-clearance

> engineer one thing: A large piece of metal is buried here. It says nothing about explosives. Muiengo sets the detector down behind him and picks up a metal probe, a foot-long tool that resembles a kitchen knife-sharpening implement. . . . As he scrapes and brushes with the precision of a surgeon, a black plastic disk appears. He knows what he's got. Or at least part of what he's got. Slightly bigger than a quarter, it's the pressure plate of an MAI-75 antipersonnel mine . . . designed to take a man's leg off below the knee. The mine has lain there, undisturbed and deadly, since it was planted five years ago.[9]

One wrong move could cost Muiengo his leg, or worse. Even the most careful, well-trained deminers are always at risk. As one human rights observer described what can happen:

> There are many dangers involved in prodding. A mine may be buried too deep for detection by a metal detector or the prod and it is discovered only with the deminer's next step. A mine can be turned on its side (either on purpose or because of natural dislocation) so that the prodder hits the pressure plate rather than the side of the mine, causing it to explode. Some mines have anti-handling devices, so that a slight disturbance will trigger its firing mechanism.[10]

Until things change, deminers will never feel completely safe at work. One is killed and two are injured for every five thousand mines lifted. A report in the *Bulletin of the American College of Surgeons* indicated that in Kuwait, which had been considered a fairly easy area to clear, "the number of deminers killed by mines since the Persian Gulf War exceeds

U.S. Marines were assigned to Lebanon as part of a multinational peacekeeping force after a confrontation between Israeli forces and the Palestine Liberation Organization.

that of U.S. military casualties [there were 383] from the conflict."[11]

One of the biggest stumbling blocks in clearing away mines is accurately detecting where they are placed. Some inexpensive land mines are so small and contain so little metal that it becomes extremely difficult for the metal detector to distinguish them from surrounding metallic debris. Completely plastic land mines are entirely missed by metal detectors.

Future Detection Methods

In recent years, there has been some research and exploratory work on improving methods of identifying buried land mines. Some of these efforts have included looking into how ground-penetrating radar (GPR) might be used to locate mines. With GPR, electromagnetic waves sent into the ground are reflected back and measured to pinpoint the precise location of buried objects. However, in identifying small objects such as antipersonnel mines (some are just three inches long), a high frequency range must be used, which sometimes registers false negatives.

Another possibility for land mine clearance might be the eventual use of infrared (IR) detection. Land mines are made of materials that tend to give off heat at a different rate than their surroundings. IR-sensing devices could measure that difference, and so would be useful in identifying land mine sites. Unfortunately, IR systems can sometimes be affected by weather conditions as well as by the size and

Members of Company A, 76th Division (Reserve), bury anti-tank/personnel mines in a field during training exercises.

makeup of the individual land mine. IR sensors also have difficulty detecting deeply buried objects.

Acoustic sensors might also be used for clearance in the years ahead. These work similarly to the sonar systems in submarines. Since sound waves transmit best in watery areas, this method would be especially useful in the heavily mined rice fields of Cambodia and Laos.

Chemical detection may become still another option for international deminers. With chemical detection, land mines are identified through the one common element they contain—explosive material. In some ways it is similar to using a dog's keen sense of smell to detect traces of explosives from land mines. A limited number of dogs have been used in some areas to find buried land mines. A canine's outstanding sense of smell enables it to be trained to detect explosives with a 95 percent success rate. But a dog is not a machine—an animal tires easily and is costly to train.

If chemical detection methods were perfected, these obstacles would be eliminated. In 1997, the United States Defense Department's Defense Advanced Research Projects Agency began a $25 million effort to develop the "electronic dog's nose program," a sensor system that imitates a dog's ability to detect land mines through its chemical makeup.

Researchers have also looked to the insect world to find new means of detection. Scientists from the University of Montana and Sandia National

A member of Company D, 864th Engineering Battalion, sweeps for mines during an Army Training and Evaluation Program (ARTEP) exercise.

Laboratories in Albuquerque, New Mexico, think that honeybees may eventually prove useful.

Tiny quantities of TNT linger in the air where there are land mines. As honeybees collect pollen in these areas, minute amounts of the substance settle on their bodies. Traces of TNT may even be present in the pollen of flowering plants as the plant absorbs the chemical from the soil.

Scientists would monitor both the bees and their hives. Detecting TNT within a hive or on a bee could mean that there are land mines in the vicinity. During testing, the bees would also be outfitted with tiny tracking devices to chart their movements. One day researchers may use honeybees to help map out possible minefields.[12]

In addition, bacteriological means of detection are also being explored for use in land mine work. This involves genetically constructing microorganisms that would recognize compounds such as explosives. Ideally, these microorganisms would be sprayed on the ground, causing areas with explosive-like compounds to produce a light or fluorescent effect. Weather and environmental conditions, however, pose significant obstacles in perfecting this technique.

Regardless of the type of improved sensor developed, engineers will also need to find a way to use it in a heavily mined zone without endangering workers. There are some vehicles that have been advertised as "mine-resistant." These have been hardened to withstand explosions, but they may not completely protect the occupants. That is why the United States

U.S. Marine Staff Sergeant Edwin Morehouse uses a metallic mine detector to locate antitank mines under the ground during demining training.

and other countries have expressed interest in robotics models and teleoperated vehicles.[13]

Such possibilities are promising, but research still has a long way to go. More effective people-friendly technology is sorely needed for the task at hand. For many people around the world, it is a matter of life or death.

4

Help

Not all who become land mine casualties are fighting a war or live in a country where land mines are planted. Sometimes those hurt by land mines come to a war-torn region to help, as did thirty-one-year-old Stig Bakkan, who joined the Norwegian United Nations peacekeeping forces when he was just nineteen years old. Initially, Bakkan joined because he wanted to see the world, but before long he realized that "securing peace for other countries was his calling and he was good at it."[1]

Injured on the Rescue

Bakkan was on his second mission to southern Lebanon in 1988 when the Norwegian United Nations patrol went out looking for those injured by a rocket attack. On the way, one of the soldiers stepped on a land mine and Bakkan and some others were sent to the rescue. Bakkan carried the stretcher while another of the peacekeepers brought the first-aid supplies. But the deminers first had to clear the site to be certain there was a safe path to the injured man. Not surprisingly, a land mine was found directly behind the man's head. Several other land mines also were found nearby. When it was believed to be safe, Bakkan and the other rescuers were finally able to lift the bleeding man onto the stretcher.

However, the moment they began to move him, another land mine suddenly exploded directly beneath Bakkan's left foot. The explosion threw him about eight meters (twenty-four feet) across the terrain. The patient on the stretcher, who was tossed into the air, landed on an adjacent riverbank. Unfortunately, Bakkan had stepped on a small plastic mine which had not been picked up by the deminers' metal detectors.

Others who were called in to stage a double rescue found Bakkan lying facedown on the ground. They immediately applied a tourniquet to his injured leg to stop the bleeding. Because they were trying to avoid other land mines near where Bakkan had been thrown, it took his rescuers nearly an hour and a half to safely put him on a stretcher and bring him to a

A U.S. Marine engineer clears land mines from a road during military training exercises.

United Nations helicopter. From there he was flown to a hospital in Haifa, Israel, where he passed out. The next morning, he awoke to find that he had only one leg.

Bakkan still misses his job on the international peacekeeping force, but now works for a Norwegian government agency that cares for neglected children. He also sometimes shares his story at conferences to raise public awareness of the dangers of land mines.[2] Fortunately, Bakkan was fitted with a prosthesis. Humanitarian groups have helped fit more land mine survivors in developing countries with these devices as well.

Cambodian Refugees

Help in some areas, like Cambodia, came slowly at first. The need was especially acute there because the widespread use of mines during the Cambodian civil war from 1979 to 1991 left the nation with the world's highest number of land mine amputees. The situation was described as follows in the article, "The Mechanical and Social Consequences of Land Mines In Cambodia," which appeared in the *Journal of the American Medical Association*:

> In the capital of Phnom Penh and nearly every major town, one encounters limbless men, women and children, with crutches tucked under their arms, begging along the roadside or in the marketplaces. Along Route 5, the war-torn strip of highway that connects Phnom Penh with the Northwest, red-colored signs warning "DANGER MINES!!" (in English and the Khmer language) line

> the edges of rice paddies and pathways. Some villagers have even placed the signs in front of their houses for "decoration" or "to keep away thieves and bad spirits."[3]

Just about anywhere in Cambodia, it is obvious that the nation has had more than its share of land mine amputees. Approximately thirty-five thousand Cambodians have lost at least one limb in a land mine accident and about three hundred new casualties occur each month. These hidden killers have cost one out of every 384 Cambodians an arm or a leg. Nearly half of all Cambodians in land mine accidents bleed to death at the explosion site. As in many other heavily mined countries, widespread poverty combined with a lack of adequate social services complicate the situation. Land mines have made Cambodia one of the world's most disabled societies.

Vietnam Veterans of America Foundation

In recent years, a number of international humanitarian relief organizations have established some vital rehabilitation programs in Cambodia and other parts of the world. In one case, such efforts were begun by a Marine veteran named Robert Muller who lost the use of his legs in combat during the Vietnam War. In 1980, Muller, along with a group of other dedicated veterans, established the Vietnam Veterans of America Foundation (VVAF) to "provide the lands where they fought with reconciliation, rehabilitation, and reconstruction."[4]

The VVAF's early humanitarian efforts centered on Southeast Asia. In 1984, Muller, accompanied by

Robert O. Muller, who lost the use of his legs in combat during the Vietnam War, has led the effort to rehabilitate victims of land mines in Southeast Asia.

other veterans, visited Cambodia and was shocked by the overwhelming number of amputees there and the low level of available rehabilitative care. The veterans wanted to help change things and set out to convince Cambodian land mine survivors that their lives could be different. "I tell these people that simply because they're disabled doesn't mean they're on the trash heap of life," Muller said in describing the veterans' approach. "The concept is so far removed from anything they've ever heard before."[5]

In 1992, the VVAF began the Kien Khleang Rehabilitation Center just outside Phnom Penh to offer rehabilitation services to land mine survivors. Other centers followed in Southeast Asia as well as in Angola and El Salvador. Since 1992, the VVAF has provided land mine amputees with more than five thousand artificial limbs, two thousand wheelchairs, and numerous orthotic braces. The VVAF served as a wheelchair provider for the United Nations Children's Fund (UNICEF) in Cambodia and supplied wheelchairs to Vietnam through the International Committee of the Red Cross.

The VVAF also offers physical therapy and the necessary follow-up services to insure proper use of the prosthetic devices for which amputees have been fitted. The VVAF was extremely innovative in bringing suitable prostheses to the regions served. It launched a workshop to make a flexible prothesis known as the Jaipur foot, which was ideal for Southeast Asia. Waterproof and shaped like a human foot, this prothesis could be worn with sandals. As the VVAF described the endeavor, "Artificial feet used in other parts of the world are not suitable for the rugged lifestyle of peasant farmers who often wear sandals or no shoes at all."[6]

Help With Job Retraining

The VVAF also works to help land mine amputees find alternative ways to earn money in their communities. In 1996, it began operating a rehabilitation skills and training center. The project, which employs local handicapped women, pays among the best wages in the area. The center also runs a silk-making operation, along with sewing, embroidery, and weaving services. Local workers support themselves and their families through the sale of scarves, vests, tote bags, hats, and other products manufactured there.

Among those who have profited from the assistance is Yor Piriy, a Cambodian woman who in 1990 stepped on a land mine while on her way to sell garlic and other food. The incident changed her life forever. She was brought to a hospital in Phnom Penh where both her legs were amputated. Piriy survived, but while recuperating she became extremely depressed over her condition and attempted suicide. It seems that after she left the hospital, she could not find work and was forced to live with her mother and two sisters. "In my mind," she explained, "I was a problem. They had to do everything for me."[7]

However, four years later, her life dramatically changed when she came to a VVAF clinic near Phnom Penh. Besides being given a wheelchair, she was hired to sew seat cushions for wheelchairs. Yor Piriy is now hopeful for the first time since her accident. "Having a job has changed my life," she said. "Now I live by myself and do not have to ask other people for money. With this job I can support my mother, sisters, and myself. They no longer support me. That is why I feel like living."[8]

Approximately 30 percent of the VVAF workforce in Cambodia is composed of individuals with disabilities, many of whom would have found it difficult to find work elsewhere. The VVAF's goal is to have the operation staffed completely by Cambodian citizens. In 1998, five Cambodians had already completed a three-year training program to become the VVAF's first certified prosthetist-orthotists. These are skilled individuals who design, create, and fix artificial limbs and braces as prescribed by a doctor. Other humanitarian groups also have begun similar efforts in pervasively land mined nations.

Clearing Land Mines in Laos

Humanitarian organizations have also sent teams of deminers into heavily mined villages and cleared them so that local residents could remain in their homes and work the land safely. Some of the efforts have centered in Laos, where, over the past twenty years, Laotians had attempted to clear their fields at great risk by picking up surfacelaid land mines and setting them aside in ravines, under bushes, or in other out-of-the-way places. As time passed, these land mines, along with numerous land mines that are still buried, have continued to disintegrate and are becoming increasingly dangerous.

However, in 1995, Laotian bomb technicians, funded by the Mennonite Central Committee (MCC) and trained by the Mines Advisory Group (MAG), traveled to a number of villages and safely exploded many of these perilous devices. One of the places they went was a village, Nanou, located in the mountainous region of Laos, where thick fertile valleys are abundant. For centuries, the area's economy relied heavily on rice farming, but now with land mines buried everywhere, the villagers' livelihood was hindered.

In January 1995, MCC/MAG bomb technicians spent a week in Nanou. By the time they left, 447 land mines and surface bombs had been destroyed. They also created a system with which residents could mark off other suspected land mine sites for the team to dispose of on their next visit. Yet the village still is not completely safe. Since no maps of the land mines planted there exist, more of these hidden killers could be anywhere. And as wind and rain erode the soil, buried land mines continue to surface. Nevertheless, the people of Nanou as well as those in other villages where the deminers have been claim to feel safer. Each destroyed land mine makes their lives a little less risky. In addition to this work at individual villages, the Laotian government also asked the MCC/MAG to demine an area encompassing more than seven school sites. This was crucial, since a land mine had already exploded in a schoolyard while the children were lining up for the morning flag salute. As in many countries plagued by land mines, an accident survey revealed that nearly half of Laotian land mine casualties (44 percent) are children under the age of fifteen. As Tavone, a Nanou girl in middle school who hopes to become a doctor, said, "Before the demolition crew came I was afraid. My brother died from a bomb."[9]

Deminer Dogs

Other groups have tried different ways to tackle the land mine problem. The Marshall Legacy Institute (MLI) joined with the Humane Society of the United States, the United Nations Development Programme, the United States Department of State, and DC Comics to come up with some innovative solutions. As part of this effort, the Marshall Legacy Institute and its partners started the K9 Demining Program. The project teams up police dogs, known as K9s, with humans from heavily mined countries to make use of a K9's remarkable ability to sniff out the explosives in land mines.

The dogs go through vigorous training to enable them to detect land mines by scent and alert their handlers to these locations. The canines and their handlers help protect many lives. Yet, while the results of this teamwork have been impressive, the price has been high. The Marshall Legacy Institute and the K9 Demining Corps break down the cost for a mine-detection dog and its training as follows:

- $1,000—$2,000 for a dog to enter explosive sniffing, mine-detection training.

- $12,000 for a specially trained explosive-sniffing dog to perform mine-detection work. This includes the cost of completing the training program and preparation for working on a team abroad.
- $40,000 for the continued training and annual operation of a mine-detection dog and its local handler. This figure covers the cost of training the handler to work with the animal effectively.

To help meet expenses, the MLI has asked for contributions toward the purchase, training, and upkeep of mine-detection dogs through its "Adopt a Dog" program. For a donation of twenty-five dollars or more, MLI will send identification tags and background information on the dog selected. For a donation of one thousand dollars or more, the MLI will send identification tags, pictures, and periodic updates on the work of that particular dog in the field.

As one of the partners in this work, the Humane Society of the United States has tried to promote awareness of the project by emphasizing the relationship of people and animals working together to make the world safer for all living things. The organization also addresses issues such as acquiring, breeding, and training mine-detection dog teams to make the program even more effective.

DC Comics, another partner in this project, uses comic books to let young people in the United States know about the vital work of the demining dog teams and to inform them of the global land mine challenge. Comic books, written in the languages of countries

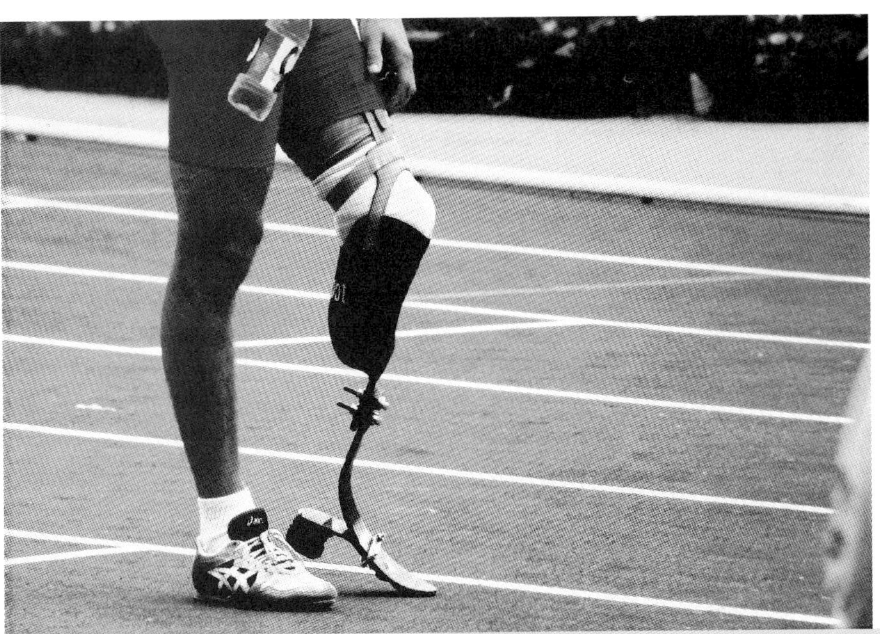

Modern technology has made it possible for those who lose a leg to walk and run almost normally—even, in some cases, to successfully run in a marathon.

where there are numerous land mines, help alert young people to the danger these killing devices pose. They also provide tips on how young people can best protect themselves from mines. The back cover of one such comic book, geared to children in Costa Rica, Honduras, and Nicaragua, noted in Spanish, "Superman and Wonder Woman have come to help the children of Central America! But even when they can't be here, you can keep yourself and others safe from land mines."[10]

Coordination of Demining Efforts

The United Nations has also been at the forefront of international efforts to resolve the global land mine crisis, and has coordinated international humanitarian demining activities. For example, the United Nations Association of the USA (UNA-USA) and the United Nations Development Programme began the Adopt-a-Minefield Program. The United Nations identifies minefields in need of clearance and UNA-USA finds potential sponsors in communities around the world to adopt these land mined areas, providing the funding to complete the task. Adopt-a-Minefield is special because it allows individuals, schools, community groups, religious organizations, businesses, and associations to help in solving the land mine problem.

The cost of clearing a minefield ranges from tens of thousands of dollars to millions of dollars, depending on the size and location of the mines. Accepting contributions as small as twenty-five dollars, UNA-USA combines the resources of smaller donors to ensure that everyone has an opportunity to participate. The program provides potential sponsors with a complete list of all available minefields, including information on location, size, and density. Potential sponsors can also learn about the anticipated demining costs, how long the project will take, and the social and economic effects minefields have had on the community.

Help From Lutheran World Relief

Lutheran World Relief (LWR) is another organization working to help land mine survivors internationally in a variety of ways. For some time, LWR has sent food, clothing, and school supplies to heavily land mined nations. Angola topped the list of countries receiving LWR assistance for several years in a row. As in many other countries, Angolan women who are injured by land mines suffer some of the worst repercussions. Often local men will not marry or even stay with an amputee, and it is extremely difficult for such women to support themselves on their own. But LWR sewing workshops have given women a chance to learn a skill. Women are given a sewing machine and a chance for a livelihood once their training is completed. For numerous Angolan land mine survivors, LWR aid has served as a stepping stone to a better life: School supplies are given to help young people learn to read; health aids are given to help families meet their medical needs; and layettes are offered to expectant mothers at prenatal classes so that they can clothe and have bedding for their newborns.

LWR's Project Comfort sends quilts and other items where they are most needed. The quilts, made by women at Lutheran churches across America, have sometimes been called "threads of compassion." The quilters spend hours cutting and sewing these items before they are sent to another part of the world.

Often quilts end up in village hospitals where land mine survivors are treated. The abject poverty and shabby conditions at these places is often all too obvious. Frequently there is a shortage of mattresses at these hospitals, and a quilt may be a patient's only source of bedding and comfort. The quilts have proven especially useful in keeping land mine survivors at these facilities warm during the winter.

Governments Work Together

Local government programs to tackle the land mine problem have been impressively effective in a number of places as well. Widespread demining efforts are being carried out in Central America. There, the numerous land mines are a sad reminder of years of regional conflicts. For decades, civil wars ravaged Nicaragua, El Salvador, and Guatemala, with border tensions frequently spilling over to affect Costa Rica and Honduras. As usual, once the conflicts were over, thousands of land mines still threatened the civilian population.

In 1991–1992, the presidents of the Central

Joao Luyaco, a father of four, stepped on a land mine and lost a leg while gathering food and medical herbs for his family.

American republics asked the Organization of American States (OAS) to initiate a program to help their national forces locate and destroy the leftover land mines. The OAS is an association of nations in the Americas that work together to foster economic, social, and military cooperation among area countries. The secretary general of the OAS, with the assistance of the Unit for the Promotion of Democracy and the expert advice of the Inter-American Defense Board, turned to member and observer governments for assistance.

Argentina, Brazil, Chile, Colombia, Peru, the United States, Uruguay, and Venezuela sent military engineers and other specialists to conduct weeks of training on mine-clearance techniques. Under the OAS-created program, these training officers teach military specialists from the host country's government how to identify and eliminate land mines. That way, the actual hands-on land mine destruction is always performed by local troops under their usual command. This is an important factor in keeping costs down.

The OAS program provides the troops with the necessary equipment to do the demining. This includes land mine detection and destruction gear with special body armor to lessen the risk of fatalities, supplementary rations, medical coverage, and life insurance. To help with these expenses, financial support has also been given by France, Germany, Japan, the Netherlands, Spain, Sweden, Switzerland, the United Kingdom, and the United States.

So far, the results have been impressive. Since

Quilts—washed and ready to keep land mine victims "under cover" while being treated in village hospitals.

demining operations began in Honduras in September 1995, thousands of acres of land have been returned to productive use. Clearing is also proceeding well in Guatemala, Costa Rica, and Nicaragua. As a result, less fertile land still lies unplanted, but in many places electrical towers, dams, and bridges are no longer left unattended.

Efforts by the United States

The United States has single-handedly spearheaded some global demining efforts. In 1997, the United States launched the Demining 2010 Initiative, which seeks to eliminate the land mine threat to civilians by 2010. To meet this goal, the United States has worked with other governments to mobilize and coordinate international support for mine clearance and survivor-aid programs.

Celebrities Speak Out

If governmental efforts have made a difference, so have the voices of prominent individuals who have spoken out against the use of land mines. At times, celebrities have used their influence to raise public awareness about the problem. Country singer Emmy Lou Harris both lobbied on Capitol Hill and gave a benefit concert for the cause, joined by Willie Nelson, Sheryl Crow, Lucinda Williams, Steve Earle, and others.

Harris first learned about the land mine crisis through a magazine article. She recalled:

> I had just read an article . . . about land mines. Like most people, I was shocked at the sheer

> magnitude of the number of land mines in the ground. . . . You don't have to take a political stance because it is a militarily irresponsible weapon that's impacting civilians around the world, most often in very poor countries. . . . It's not enough to say we won't put any more in the ground, we've got to get them out. It comes down to basic courtesy, something you learn in kindergarten: You clean up after your mess when you're through. Until we do, these countries are going to be hostages. They're going to continue to live the war many many years after peace has been declared.[11]

The Influence of Royalty

Royalty has also focused attention on the plight of land mine casualties. Before her death in 1997, Diana, Princess of Wales, visited both Angola and Bosnia on British Red Cross missions. At the time, much of the British population as well as that of the United States were unaware of the hardships caused by land mines. Diana's stays in these countries, and her visits to hospitals, rehabilitation centers, and other sites provided millions with actual images of the devastation. In a speech following her tours, she addressed the tremendous human suffering caused by these weapons, which greatly increased public knowledge of this issue. A few months later, Britain's government banned all British trade in these weapons and promised to destroy its own land mine stocks by 2005.

Her Majesty Queen Noor of Jordan has also lent her voice to the movement to ban land mines. In July

1998, she summed up their lingering menace when she noted, "Even in long-hoped-for peace, these insidious leftovers [land mines] are a bitter reminder of past conflict and a threat to future progress. War-torn societies can never be rebuilt so long as a single step on mine-infested ground can be fatal."[12]

Survivors Speak Out

Yet, while famous voices have drawn attention to this important cause, some of the most moving pleas for action have come from those whose lives were forever changed by these indiscriminate weapons. Chris Moon is a land mine survivor who runs marathons to call attention to the plight of international land mine survivors, and also raises money to assist them.

Moon was injured when he stepped on a land mine in 1995 in northern Mozambique while working for the Halo Trust, a British-based mine clearance agency. But he does not consider himself a victim. "I chose to work in a mine-infested area. The people living in such areas do not have the same choice," Moon says.[13] Having lost the lower part of his right arm and his right leg below the knee, Moon runs wearing a prosthesis.

Moon recently completed a marathon in Oslo, Norway, in his fastest time ever, despite some problems with his artificial limb. Although other disabled athletes ran part of the course, Moon was one of the few to complete the marathon. Having raised a sizable sum from T-shirt sales and donations to the run,

Moon earmarked the money for children injured by land mines in Grozny, Chechnya.

Less than a year after his accident, Moon successfully ran the London Marathon in just over five and a half hours. That was the start of his campaign to help those disabled by land mines. Since that time, Moon has raised money for the injured by running in Sweden, Cambodia, Mozambique, the United States, France, and Australia.

Moon was also the first amputee to complete the Great Sahara Run. This was especially challenging since the race takes place over the course of a week and covers 150 miles through the sand and heat of the Sahara Desert. All participating runners were required to carry their own food, clothing, and gear throughout the marathon. "Many people told me it would not be possible to complete the run on a false limb, but I finished 281 out of 360 participants," Moon noted. "We managed to raise over $130,000 for a prothesis program."[14]

Abraham Gabreyesus, from Eritrea, is another land mine survivor who has effectively spoken out for improved aid for people throughout the world disabled by land mines. Gabreyesus's tragic land mine encounter occurred when he was just a boy. He recalled:

> My older sister would warn me every day not to play near the mines and not to touch anything metal in the ground. I was eleven years old and I would tell her I could take care of myself. She did not have to worry, I was not a child.

> It had been five months since the fighting in my village had stopped and the soldiers moved on. I was playing in a field with friends when I found what I thought was a small battery. I was curious and removed it from the ground. I hit it with a stone three times, on the third, it exploded.[15]

Gabreyesus's treatment was not unlike that of many land mine survivors in developing countries. He was taken by cart to a hospital about four hours away. The explosion had a devastating effect on his eyes, and in the end the boy lost his vision and one arm. Gabreyesus said:

> The full consequences of what happened did not hit me until I returned to my village. I could no longer play with my friends, nor could I go to school with them. I loved to learn and tried learning orally from my brothers when they would return home from school. Later, I tried going to school and listening and memorizing but this was not working. It was very difficult and very painful for me.[16]

About two years after the accident, some of his relatives in the city helped Gabreyesus to attend a school for the blind there. "This was a very happy time for me," he said. "I was learning Braille and was among people with the same problems as me." Knowing Braille made it possible for him to return to his village school after a while. Braille textbooks supplied by the school for the blind allowed him to keep up with his lessons. As a result, Gabreyesus graduated with honors, attended college, and eventually went on to law school. At the time this book was published, he was twenty-six years old.

While at a land mine conference, Gabreyesus met Rae McGrath, the former director of the Mines Advisory Group, a humanitarian demining organization. McGrath arranged for Gabreyesus to go to some doctors who believed the young man's vision might be restored through an operation. McGrath raised the money for the surgery and at a later conference in Johannesburg, Gabreyesus met the surgeon general of South Africa, who arranged for him to have the procedure.

As Gabreyesus described his good fortune:

> I received a corneal transplant and lens implantation in my right eye and received an artificial arm. I can see again. How different my life would have been if I could have had access to such medical care when I was first injured.
>
> What has been made available to me should be available to all land mine victims regardless of where they live or how much money they have. We have the medical and educational technology and we have the victims. What is needed is the political will and NGO [nongovernmental organization] focus to bring the two together.[17]

Gabreyesus firmly believes that a single international institution devoted solely to meeting the medical and educational needs of land mine survivors must be formed. Frequently he points to his own case to explain why. "Medical experts, educators, governments, and aid workers all worked together to help me. All survivors should have the same chance," he again stressed. Gabreyesus added:

> For me there is little value in the process [of banning land mines] without support for survivor assistance. The problem of victims is not simply the victims' problem. It is a problem for the community. . . . Even politicians and activists that speak loudly for a [land mine] ban sometimes forget the survivors.[18]

Gabreyesus's experience and words are a reminder that the needs of land mine survivors must be addressed.

5

A Treaty to Ban Land Mines

Land mines have sometimes been described as weapons of mass destruction that act in slow motion. Yet, while treaties exist to stop the use of more obvious weapons of mass destruction, such as chemical, biological, and nuclear armaments, until the 1990s no agreements specifically banned land mines.

Convention on Conventional Weapons

Nevertheless, there were some attempts at regulation, including the 1980 Convention on Conventional Weapons (CCW), an international humanitarian law treaty. The CCW attempts to regulate land mines through its Land Mine Protocol (Protocol II). The United States played a significant role in completing the CCW's Amended Mine Protocol in 1996, which significantly strengthened restrictions on land mine use and transfer.

However, many felt that the Convention on Conventional Weapons still failed to adequately address the humanitarian crisis caused by land mines. Because more land mines are planted daily than removed, humanitarian groups decided that an international treaty to ban land mines altogether was imperative. Clearly, a worldwide campaign to bring about this goal would have to be launched.

International Campaign to Ban Land Mines

In 1991, the Vietnam Veterans of America Foundation and Medico International (a German-based humanitarian aid group) founded the International Campaign to Ban Land Mines (ICBL). VVAF hired Jody Williams, ICBL's principal coordinator since its beginning, to organize the campaign. Williams had written extensively on land mines and lectured throughout the world on this problem. With so many people still unaware of the horrific effects of land mines, the challenge ahead seemed daunting. Everyone involved knew that success had not come easily in the past. Nevertheless, some positive steps were taking place.

In 1991, Vermont Senator Patrick Leahy and

Illinois Representative Lane Evans introduced a bill containing a moratorium banning United States exports of antipersonnel land mines for one year. Later passed by Congress, the Leahy/Evans moratorium was "the first legislation of its kind anywhere in the world."[1] In 1993, Senator Leahy introduced legislation extending the United States moratorium, which passed the Senate by a unanimous vote.

Meanwhile, the ICBL had continued to raise public awareness about the plight of land mine survivors. In 1992, the VVAF, Medico International, Human Rights Watch, Physicians for Human Rights, the Mines Advisory Group, and Handicap International formed ICBL's first steering committee. These were all international humanitarian groups that wanted to see things change. Although the first international conference on land mines in 1992 in New York City drew only six nongovernmental organizations, the ICBL has since grown to more than one thousand organizations in sixty nations. "The support for a ban didn't come out of nowhere," Williams said. "Hundreds of organizations were involved in the issue in the field. There was a national constituency to pull together."[2]

Williams also worked with officials from various nations to gain support for an international treaty to ban land mines.

Conference in Canada

Canada took an important leadership role in this process. Eager for a successful outcome, the

Canadian government hosted a conference in October 1996 in which a politically binding statement known as the Ottawa Declaration was adopted and an agenda for action drawn up. At the close of the conference, Canadian Foreign Minister Lloyd Axworthy issued an invitation to all governments to return to Ottawa in December 1997 to sign a treaty to completely prohibit land mines.

Williams later described the reaction to Axworthy's invitation:

> But the Foreign Minister did not end with congratulations. He ended with a challenge. The Canadian government challenged the world to return to Canada in a year to sign an international treaty banning antipersonnel land mines. Members of the ICBL erupted into cheers. The silence of the governments in the room was deafening. Even the truly pro-ban states were horrified by the challenge. Canada had stepped outside the diplomatic process and procedure and put them between a rock and a hard place. They had said they were pro-ban. What could they do? They had to respond. It was really breathtaking.[3]

Two months after the Ottawa Conference, the United States offered a resolution in the United Nations General Assembly calling for a new, legally binding treaty banning the production, use, stockpiling, and transfer of antipersonnel mines, to be concluded as soon as possible. The resolution was supported by 156 nations with none against.

But the Ottawa Process was a fast-track route outside of the usual United Nations disarmament procedure, and many involved felt that there was no

Canadian Foreign Minister Lloyd Axworthy spearheaded the attempt to rid the world of land mines, which began at the Ottawa Conference in December 1997.

time to lose on this issue. The following year, the long-awaited moment finally came. In December 1997, 124 nations signed the international treaty to ban land mines. Axworthy said, in commenting on the momentous event, "The effort to ban AP mines is an example of the democratization of foreign policy decisions, a true partnership between governments, nongovernmental organizations, international agencies, and millions of citizens around the world."[4]

Nobel Peace Prize Awarded

The ICBL had a banner year in 1997. The organization and Jody Williams were jointly awarded the Nobel Peace Prize. Accepting the award on behalf of the ICBL was a Cambodian land mine survivor named Tun Channareth, whose legs were shattered in a minefield about fifteen years earlier. Channareth's land mine encounter occurred in December 1982, shortly after he had been called up for military service, and was traveling with a group of soldiers.

Channareth recalled:

> Our group of soldiers had managed to get halfway up to our destination when we came across a mined area. I stepped on a mine and both my legs were rendered useless by the explosion. Stripped of all my weapons, I was left to die alone in the forest. I was later found by two members of a reconnaissance party. I dragged myself across the minefield and was quickly put into a hammock.

Having lost a large amount of blood and drifting in and out of consciousness, Channareth was finally taken to a hospital. "I remember the doctor, with tears in his eyes, telling me he would have to amputate my legs," the former soldier continued. "I wanted nothing more than to return home . . . to die."[5]

But Channareth did not die. Instead he learned new skills and became a talented wheelchair designer as well as an active campaigner for the ICBL. Channareth helped to launch a petition that received more than five hundred thousand signatures in favor of the land mine ban. While working to win over others to the cause, he met with Cambodia's king, the Pope, the queen of Spain, and the president of Ireland. He also addressed the British Parliament.

Channareth's eloquent acceptance speech at the Nobel awards ceremony summed up the universal responsibility to wholeheartedly support the ban against land mines. Channareth said:

> Some people call me a land mine victim. So I am. So are you in a different way. You can see I carry in my body the injury caused by land mines. Forty thousand people look like me. Many, many more have lost arms or eyes or one leg. Many, too, still carry pieces of shrapnel in their bodies causing them suffering and new medical expenses for years. Others carry the emotional scars, the memory of loved ones killed, the sense of being useless, no good, maimed. . . . Remember this: We are all land mine victims when we allow this system to continue, when we refuse to ban, to demine, to assist communities and people suffering. . . . Together, we can stop a coward's war that makes victims of us all.[6]

Williams's reaction to sharing the award was one of joy and exhilaration. "Yippee!" she exclaimed. "The

Nobel Prize is formal recognition that the campaign changed the world in a breathtakingly short period of time." Nevertheless, there is still much more to do.

Arguments in Favor of Land Mines

A number of nations have not yet signed the Mine Ban Treaty. Israel argues that it needs land mines because of terrorist activity within its borders. According to Israeli Ambassador David Sultan,

> Due to our unique situation in the Middle East involving an ongoing threat of hostilities as well as terrorist threats . . . we are still obligated to maintain antipersonnel land mines as necessary for self-defense . . . to ensure the protection of civilians threatened on a daily basis by terrorists and to ensure the protection of Israeli forces operating in areas of armed conflict.[7]

Egypt also says that it must use land mines to defend against terrorism. In addition, the country has stated that land mines serve as an important means of reducing drug trafficking along its borders. The Egyptian government also says it regrets the fact that the treaty does not make the countries who use mines in various parts of the world responsible for removing these devices. Millions of mines were buried in Egypt during World War II by German, Italian, and British forces.

The Federal Republic of Yugoslavia has not signed the treaty, either. A land mine expert on the general staff of the Yugoslav military defended their policy by saying, "Considering the fact that the Yugoslav military doctrine is primarily defensive, antipersonnel and antitank land mines have a very important place in our defensive system."[8] But, of course, weapons can also be used offensively in combat.

The Russian Federation has not signed the Mine Ban Treaty, although former president Boris Yeltsin and other officials have stated that it intends to do so sometime in the future. Among the reasons cited for the signing delay are that Russia was not financially able to demolish its huge stockpile of land mines within four years as specified in the treaty. Colonel-General Vladimir P. Kuznetsov, then Chief Commander of the Engineer Forces, also said that Russia could not sign the treaty because there are still no available "alternative means that could adequately substitute for APMs [antipersonnel mines] and fulfill their military task."[9]

China is still another country that has refused to sign. The Chinese government believes that land mines are necessary to protect its extensive borders. It also stressed that, as a developing country, China lacks both the financial means and technology to replace mines with more advanced defensive weapons.

The United States Has Not Signed Treaty

A number of other countries also have not signed the treaty, among them the United States. Before the treaty existed, the United States had taken an active leadership role in attempting to rid the world of antipersonnel land mines. In his 1994 address to the United Nations General Assembly, President Bill

Clinton was the first world leader to call for an antipersonnel land mine ban. In addition, the United States had provided humanitarian demining assistance to heavily mined nations since 1993 and substantially broadened these efforts since. By 1998, the United States provided humanitarian demining assistance amounting to nearly $92 million to twenty-one countries in Asia, Africa, Central America, and eastern Europe.

Hundreds of highly qualified United States military and civilian personnel have trained thousands of local deminers in various nations. They have offered instruction in such areas as mine awareness, mine clearance techniques, emergency medical care, and how to establish a national mine action center. Besides this assistance, the United States has contributed funding for the research and development of enhanced mechanical and technical applications for mine detection and clearance, and has sponsored various survivor medical programs.

President Clinton claimed that the United States did not sign the treaty because it did not contain an exemption required by the United States to protect its servicemen in Korea. Unfortunately, a tense, potentially volatile situation still exists along the border of North and South Korea. The Pentagon claims that land mines are a key component of South Korea's defense against an invasion from the North. The South Korean government underscored the need for land mines, noting:

> The use of APLs [antipersonnel land mines] on the Korean peninsula has been an essential element in

> deterring possible aggression. It has helped prevent the recurrence of another devastating war. . . . Mining along the north-south invasion routes would work to slow down and break up a North Korean attack. . . . Minefields have also been an indispensable component of our defensive barrier system. . . . APLs have thus served as a powerful deterrent to military adventurism in Korea and will continue to do so.[10]

United States Military Debates Land Mines

Though President Clinton supported the Pentagon's official position on land mines in Korea, for some time there has been a difference of opinion within the military as to whether land mines should ever be used anywhere. David H. Hackworth, a journalist and one of America's most decorated soldiers, who served in World War II, Korea, and Vietnam, believes that the United States armed forces used mines irresponsibly in Vietnam, dropping millions of them randomly by air. Hackworth noted:

> The enemy quickly learned how to disarm these weapons and recycle them for use against us. The infantry battalion I commanded in the Ninth Division took more than 1,800 casualties in a year and a half, most of them caused by recycled U.S. ordnance. Mines cannot secure a flank or defend a position by themselves. . . . Mines never stopped any unit of mine from taking its objective—or the enemy from getting inside my wire. . . . Most serving generals, especially the desk jockeys, are in favor of mines. The real war-fighters usually

> want to get rid of them. . . . They are ugly, ineffective weapons and they ought to be outlawed.[11]

Army documents contained in the Human Rights Watch/VVAF report, entitled "In Its Own Words," underscored those sentiments, revealing the following data on land mine use in Vietnam and Korea:

- More United States Army mine casualties in Korea were caused by U.S. defensive minefields than by the enemy's mines.
- The main sources of land mines for the enemy in both Korea and Vietnam were captured United States mines and mine components.
- In Korea, 100,000 United States mines out of a shipment of 120,000 were lost to the enemy.
- United States minefields were easily breached during the Korean War, sending United States troops retreating through their own unmarked minefields.

"After the release of 'In Its Own Words,' there should be no foundation left for those who want to argue that we should fight to hold on to such weapons," retired Lieutenant General James Hollingsworth argued.[12] Hollingsworth, who commanded United States forces in Korea from 1973 to 1976, believes the president should sign the land mine ban treaty. Retired army generals Henry (Hank) Emerson, David Palmer, and Douglas Kinnard, among others, agree.

"I have always been convinced that land mines caused more harm than good in Korea," charged

Members of Company A, 76th Division (Reserve), arm anti-tank/personnel mines during training exercises.

retired Lieutenant General Emerson, who was twice awarded the Distinguished Service Cross as well as five Silver Stars and two Purple Hearts. "I know a significant number of the land mines we encountered in Vietnam were of U.S. origin. They are a horrible weapon and they caused a very high proportion of our casualties in Vietnam."[13] Retired Lieutenant General Palmer's comment was, "I never saw a situation where I thought the use of antipersonnel land mines would be wise militarily for American forces, nor can I envision one in theory."[14]

Although anti–land mine activists and others want President Clinton to heed these arguments and sign the treaty immediately, that seems unlikely. However, in May 1998, the Clinton administration did announce a policy shift that commits the United States to find alternatives to land mines and to sign the international treaty to ban land mines by the year 2006.

Treaty Signed in 1999

Meanwhile, the treaty went into effect without the world's last superpower signing it. After it was officially ratified by the governments of at least forty countries, it officially began on March 1, 1999. By that time, 134 nations had signed the treaty, 65 had ratified it, and 12 countries had already destroyed their entire stock of land mines. To mark the official start of the treaty, there were ceremonies, celebrations, and the ringing of church bells around the world. Children's choirs sang, and balloons and doves were released into the air.

Yet despite the jubilance, many anti–land mine activists believe their work will not be done until the world is free of land mines. One key goal is having the United States sign and ratify the treaty. "The signing's extraordinary, but it's at risk of becoming a hollow treaty if the U.S. isn't brought on board," VVAF founder Robert Muller said. "It's ironic and sad that this country, which played so important a part in getting this campaign off the ground is, at the end of the day, a no-show."[15]

Muller's sentiments were echoed by many who felt that the United States should have signed the treaty. As a *USA Today* editorial pointed out: "The U.S. has joined a few nations, including rogue states like Iran and Iraq, on the outside of a remarkable process."[16] Longtime anti–land mine proponent Senator Patrick Leahy said in his address to the United States Senate,

> President Clinton and I have spoken many times about the land mine issue and I am convinced that he wants to see these weapons banned . . . but . . . I am just as convinced that a tremendous opportunity was lost last week [when the U.S. did not sign the treaty]—an opportunity that rarely comes in history.[17]

Campaign for a Land Mine-Free World

After the treaty was signed, the VVAF established the Campaign for a Land Mine–Free World in 1998 to provide post-Ottawa leadership in three areas: humanitarian assistance to victims, demining, and public education. Existing humanitarian programs will be upgraded as well as extended to other war-torn regions of the world. The VVAF will conduct a precisely targeted survey of twelve of the most heavily mined countries to help humanitarian demining agencies prioritize their work more efficiently. It will also continue raising public awareness on the land mine crisis to encourage the United States to sign the Ottawa Treaty as soon as possible. The work ahead is crucial because, as too many people have already learned, "Wars end, but land mines don't."[18] A doctor who has treated numerous land mine victims perhaps best summed up the imperative when he said, "Even for a veteran war surgeon, looking at the body of a child torn to pieces by these inhumane weapons is startling and upsetting. This carnage has nothing to do with military strategy. It is a deliberate choice to inflict monstrous pain and mutilation. It is a crime against humanity."[19]

Appendix

Key Provisions in the 1997 Treaty Banning Land Mines

Convention on the Prohibition of the Use, Stockpiling, Production, and Transfer of Anti-Personnel Mines and on Their Destruction—September 18, 1997—Final Text, Oslo, Norway.

Open for signature, December 3, 1997, Ottawa, Canada.

ARTICLE 1

General Obligations

1. Each State Party undertakes never under any circumstances:
   a) To use antipersonnel mines;
   b) To develop, produce, otherwise acquire, stockpile, retain or transfer to anyone, directly or indirectly, antipersonnel mines;
   c) To assist, encourage or induce, in any way, anyone to engage in any activity prohibited to a State Party under this Convention.
2. Each State Party undertakes to destroy or ensure the destruction of all antipersonnel mines in accordance with the prohibitions of this Convention.

ARTICLE 4

Destruction of Stockpiled Antipersonnel Mines

Except as provided for in Article 3 [for training purposes], each State Party undertakes to destroy or ensure the destruction of all stockpiled antipersonnel mines it owns or possesses, or that are under its jurisdiction or control, as soon as possible but not later than four years after the entry into force of this Convention for that State Party.

ARTICLE 5

Destruction of Antipersonnel Mines in Mined Areas

1. Each State Party undertakes to destroy or ensure the destruction of all antipersonnel mines in mined areas under its jurisdiction or control, as soon as possible but not later than ten years after the entry into force of this Convention for that State Party.
2. Each State Party shall make every effort to identify all areas under its jurisdiction or control in which antipersonnel mines are known or suspected to be emplaced and shall ensure as soon as possible that all antipersonnel mines in mined areas under its jurisdiction or control are perimeter-marked, monitored, and protected by fencing or other means, to ensure the effective exclusion of civilians, until all antipersonnel mines contained therein have been destroyed. The marking shall at least be to the standards set out in the Protocol on Prohibitions or Restrictions on the Use of Mines, Booby Traps, and Other Devices as amended on 3 May 1996, annexed to the Convention on Prohibitions or Restrictions on the Use of Certain Conventional Weapons Which May Be Deemed to Be Excessively Injurious or to Have Indiscriminate Effects.
3. If a State Party believes that it will be unable to destroy or ensure the destruction of all antipersonnel mines referred to in paragraph 1 within that time period, it may submit a request to a Meeting of the States Parties or a Review Conference for an extension of the deadline for completing the destruction of such antipersonnel mines, for a period of up to ten years.

ARTICLE 7

Transparency Measures

1. Each State Party shall report to the Secretary-General of the United Nations as soon as practicable, and in any event not later than 180 days after the entry into force of this Convention for that State Party, on:
   a) The national implementation measures;
   b) The total of all stockpiled antipersonnel mines owned or possessed by it, or under its jurisdiction or control, to include a breakdown of the type, quantity, and, if possible, lot numbers of each type of antipersonnel mine stockpiled;
   c) To the extent possible, the location of all mined areas that contain, or are suspected to contain, antipersonnel mines under its jurisdiction or control, to include as much detail as possible regarding the type and quantity of each type of anti-personnel mine in each mined area and when they were emplaced;
   d) The types, quantities and, if possible, lot numbers of all antipersonnel mines retained or transferred for the development of and training in mine detection, mine clearance, or mine destruction techniques, or transferred for the purpose of destruction, as well as the institutions authorized by a State Party to retain or transfer antipersonnel mines, in accordance with Article 3.

ARTICLE 12

Review Conferences

A Review Conference shall be convened by the Secretary-General of the United Nations five years after the entry into force of this Convention. Further Review Conferences shall be convened by the Secretary-General of the United Nations if so requested by one or more State Parties, provided that the interval between Review Conferences shall in no case be less than five years. All State Parties shall be invited to each Review Conference.

ARTICLE 19

Reservations

The Articles of this Convention shall not be subject to reservations.

ARTICLE 20

1. This Convention shall be of unlimited duration.

SOURCE: Physicians For Human Rights, *Record*, April 1998.

Chapter Notes

Chapter 1. Remnants of War

1. Scott Canon, "Fear of Mines Likely to Haunt Kosovo for Many Years," Knight-Ridder/Tribune News Service, June 14, 1999, p. K4930.

2. Ibid.

3. Ibid.

4. *Land Mines: Fallout of War*, Office of Global Education/Church World Service, Baltimore, Md., p. 2.

5. Elias Issac, *Anti-Personnel Land Mines in Angola,* The Division of Overseas Ministries of Global Ministries, Indianapolis, Ind. n.p., n.d.

6. *Hidden Killers*, Office of Humanitarian Demining, U.S. Department of State, Bureau of Political-Military Affairs, Washington, D.C., September 3, 1998, p. 13.

7. *Toward a Mine-Free Southern Africa*, A Report from the Fourth International NGO Conference on Land Mines, Maputo, Mozambique, February 24–28, 1997.

8. UNICEF's "The State of the World's Children" Web site, October 15, 1995, <http://www.unicef.org/sowc96pk/hidekill.htm> October 20, 1999.

9. *Land Mines: Fallout of War*, p. 1.

10. Ibid.

11. *Hidden Killers*, p. iii.

12. *Land Mines: Fallout of War,* p. 2.

13. *Bureau for Global Programs Fund—Cambodia, Laos & Vietnam*, U.S. Agency for International Development, Office of Health and Nutrition, 1998, n.p.

14. *Secret War: Continuing Tragedy*, Mennonite Central Committee, n.p., n.d.

15. *Land Mines: A Deadly Legacy*, The Arms Project and Physicians for Human Rights (New York: Human Rights Watch, 1993), p. 226.

16. Rae McGrath and Eric Stover, "Injuries From Land Mines," *British Medical Journal*, December 14, 1991, p. 303.

17. Mary-Anne Anderson, "Taking Action: The War on Land Mines," *Red Cross, Red Crescent: The Magazine of the International Red Cross and Red Crescent Movement*, Issue 2, 1997, p. 2.

18. Statement of Senator Patrick Leahy, *Congressional Record*, July 22, 1993, p. S 290.

19. Pearl Sensenig, *Laos: War Legacy*, Mennonite Central Committee and MCC U.S., Akron, Pa.: 1994, p. 9.

20. Ibid., p. 21.

21. Paul Davies, *War of the Mines: Cambodia, Land Mines and the Impoverishment of a Nation* (Boulder, Colo.: Pluto Press, 1994), p. 74.

22. *Toward a Mine-Free Southern Africa*.

23. Ibid.

24. James C. Cobey, M.D., Eric Stover, and Jonathan Fine, "Civilian Injuries Due to War Mines," *Techniques in Orthopedics*, vol. 10, no. 3, Fall 1995, p. 261.

25. Ibid.

26. Eric Stover, Allen S. Keller M.D., James C. Cobey, M.D., and Sam Sopheap, "The Medical and Social Consequences of Land Mines in Cambodia," *Journal of the American Medical Association*, vol. 272, no. 5, August 3, 1994, p. 332.

27. Davies, p. 72.

28. Stover, Keller, Cobey, and Sopheap, p. 333.

29. Sheri Prasso, "The Misery Here is Just Phenomenal," *Business Week*, October 6, 1997, p. 148.

30. *The State of the World's Refugees, 1997–98*, United Nations High Commission for Refugees, A Humanitarian Agenda, 1997, p. 268.

Chapter 2. The Killing Fields

1. Kathryn Wolford, "Deadly Harvest," *The Christian Century*, April 24, 1996, p. 444.

2. Philip C. Winslow, *Sowing the Dragon's Teeth: Land Mines and the Global Legacy of War* (Boston: Beacon Press, 1997), p. 13.

3. Rae McGrath and Eric Stover, *Land Mines in Cambodia: The Coward's War* (Asia Watch and Physicians for Human Rights Reports, September 1991), p. 43.

4. James C. Cobey, M.D., "Mechanical Complications of Antipersonnel Land Mines," *Bulletin of the American College of Surgeons*, vol. 81, no. 8, August 1996, p. 10.

5. Winslow, p. 136.

6. *The Casualties Don't Stop When the War Does*, Physicians Against Land Mines, Chicago. n.p., n.d.

Chapter 3. The Comings and Goings of Land Mines

1. "A Mine Producer's Repentance," *International Campaign to Ban Land Mines: Report on Activities* (Washington, D.C.: Vietnam Veterans of America Foundation, 1997), p. 66.

2. Ibid.

3. *Land Mines: A Deadly Legacy*, The Arms Project and Physicians for Human Rights (New York: Human Rights Watch, 1993), p. 37.

4. *The Basics*, an informational sheet compiled by Global Ministries, United Church Board for World Ministries, Cleveland, Ohio.

5. Ibid.

6. *Land Mines: A Deadly Legacy*, p. 235.

7. *Why They Don't Make Sense*, an informational sheet compiled by Global Ministries, United Church Board for World Ministries, Cleveland, Ohio.

8. *Hidden Killers*, Office of Humanitarian Demining, U.S. Department of State, Bureau of Political-Military Affairs, Washington, D.C., September 3, 1998, p. 99.

9. Philip C. Winslow, *Sowing the Dragon's Teeth: Land Mines and the Global Legacy of War* (Boston: Beacon Press, 1997), p. 8.

10. Eric Stover, Allen S. Keller, M.D., James C. Cobey, M.D., and Sam Sopheap, "The Medical and Social Consequences of Land Mines in Cambodia," *Journal of the American Medical Association*, vol. 272, no. 5, August 3, 1994, p. 334.

11. James C. Cobey, M.D., "Mechanical Complications of Antipersonnel Land Mines," *Bulletin of the American College of Surgeons*, vol. 81, no. 8, August 1996, p. 10.

12. "Can Bees Take the Sting Out of Land Mines?," *Business Week*, June 7, 1999, p. 137.

13. *Hidden Killers*, p. 105.

Chapter 4. Help

1. Kamel Saadi, "A Norwegian Peacekeeper's Tale of Courage," *International Campaign to Ban Land Mines: Report on Activities* (Washington, D.C.: Vietnam Veterans of America Foundation, 1997), p. 56.

2. Ibid.

3. Eric Stover, Allen S. Keller, M.D., James Cobey, M.D., and Sam Sopheap, "The Medical and Social Consequences of Land Mines in Cambodia," *Journal of the American Medical Association*, vol. 272, no. 5, August 3, 1994, p. 332.

4. *Global Visions, Concrete Solutions*, Vietnam Veterans of America Foundation, Annual Report, 1997, p. 4.

5. Susan Reed, "A Marine's Reparation," *People Weekly*, December 11, 1995, p. 103.

6. *Global Visions, Concrete Solutions*, p. 6.

7. *Campaign for a Land Mine Free World-Turning Tragedy into Hope*, Vietnam Veterans of America Foundation, 1997.

8. Ibid.

9. *Laos: Safe Villages*, The Mennonite Central Committee, Akron, Pa., 1995, p. 16.

10. Eduardo Barreto, *The Hidden Killer* (New York: DC Comics, 1998), comic book, back cover.

11. Richard Harrington, "A Disarming Performance," *The Washington Post*, October 9, 1998, p. 11.

12. *Land Mine Monitor: An Introduction*, International Campaign to Ban Land Mines, December 1998, p. 11.

13. "Moon Runs For Chechnya," *International Campaign to Ban Land Mines: Report on Activities* (Washington, D.C.: Vietnam Veterans of America Foundation, 1997), p. 66.

14. Ibid.

15. "Campaigner Profile: Abraham Gabreyesus," *International Campaign to Ban Land Mines: Report on Activities* (Washington, D.C.: Vietnam Veterans of America Foundation, 1997), p. 57.

16. Ibid.

17. Ibid.

18. Ibid.

Chapter 5. A Treaty to Ban Land Mines

1. *Global Visions, Concrete Solutions*, Vietnam Veterans of America Foundation, Annual Report, 1997, p. 14.

2. D'Arcey Jenish, "Landing the Prize: Peace Activists Share the 1997 Nobel," *MacLean's*, October 20, 1997, p. 32.

3. Jody Williams, "The 1997 Nobel Peace Prize Lectures," Physicians For Human Rights, *Record*, April 1998, p. 7.

4. Lloyd Axworthy, "In This Issue of Red Cross, Red Crescent," *Red Cross, Red Crescent: The Magazine of the International Red Cross and Red Crescent Movement*, Issue 2, 1997, p. 1.

5. "Tun Channareth's Road To Ottawa," *International Campaign to Ban Land Mines: Report on Activities* (Washington, D.C.: Vietnam Veterans of America Foundation, 1997), p. 26.

6. Tun Channareth, "Blossoming the Tree of Peace," Physicians for Human Rights, *Record*. April 1998, p. 11.

7. David H. Hackworth, "One Weapon We Don't Need," *Newsweek*, April 8, 1996, p. 29.

8. "Retired Generals Renew Call for Total Antipersonnel Mine Ban," *International Campaign to Ban Land Mines: Report on Activities* (Washington, D.C.: Vietnam Veterans of America Foundation, 1997), p. 26.

9. Ibid., p. 27.

10. Ibid.

11. Hackworth, p. 29.

12. "Retired Generals Renew Call for Total Antipersonnel Mine Ban," p. 26.

13. Ibid., p. 27.

14. Ibid.

15. Jenish.

16. Frances X. Clines, "28-Year Quest to Abolish Land Mines Pays Off for Veteran Who Fights On," *The New York Times*, December 3, 1997, p. 10A.

17. "The Land Mine Ban Treaty: A Lost Chance For Leadership," An Address to the U.S. Senate by Senator Patrick Leahy, *Congressional Record*, September 23, 1997, pp. 9778–9781.

18. *Global Visions*, *Concrete Solutions*, p. 15.

19. Gino Strada, "The Horror of Land Mines," *Scientific American*, May 1996, p. 45.

Glossary

antipersonnel land mines—Encased explosive devices usually placed beneath the ground or, in some instances, on or near the ground. Antipersonnel land mines are designed to hurt people rather than destroy military vehicles.

antitank land mines—Land mines designed to blow up army tanks and other military vehicles. Antitank mines contain higher levels of explosives than antipersonnel mines and are geared to be triggered by military vehicles.

clearance—Removal of land mines from a defined area.

Demining 2010 Initiative—An effort launched by the United States to eliminate the land mine threat to civilians by the year 2010.

detection—Discovering or confirming a land mine's precise location.

humanitarian demining—Activity associated with improving or eliminating the land mine problem in a given nation.

Jaipur foot—A waterproof artificial foot shaped like a human foot that can be worn with sandals, which makes it ideal for amputees living in Southeast Asia.

Mine Action Center (MAC)—A facility that coordinates and assists demining and survivor-assistance efforts in a nation.

Ottawa Process—The fast-track diplomatic initiative signed in December 1997 that led to the creation of an international treaty to ban land mines.

ordnance—Military supplies, including weapons.

orthotist—A doctor or scientist who studies joints or muscles.

prosthesis—An artificial limb used by an amputee.

prosthetist-orthotist—A skilled person who designs, creates, and fits artificial limbs, braces, and other appliances as prescribed by a physician.

survivor assistance—Any activity geared to restoring land mine survivors to a productive life and livelihood, including the return and resettlement of refugees, medical rehabilitation of individuals, and training or retraining in civilian pursuits.

tourniquet—A tightly tied noose-like bandage to control bleeding.

Further Reading

Books

Aaseng, Nathan. *You Are the General*. Minneapolis, Minn.: The Oliver Press, 1994.

Africa Watch. *Land Mines in Angola*. New York: Human Rights Watch, 1993.

Cahill, Kevin, ed. *Clearing the Fields: Solutions to the Global Land Mine Crisis*. New York: Basic Books, 1994.

Croll, Mike. *The History of Land Mines*. Barnsley, England: Leo Cooper, 1998.

Davies, Paul. *War of the Mines: Cambodia, Land Mines and the Improvement of a Nation*. Boulder, Colo.: Pluto Press, 1994.

Roberts, Shawn and Jody Williams. *After the Guns Fall Silent: The Enduring Legacy of Land Mines*. Sterling, Va.: Oxfam Publishing, 1995.

Roleff, Tarmava, ed. *War: Opposing Viewpoints*. San Diego, Calif.: Greenhaven Press, 1999.

Wikesser, Carol, ed. *America's Defense: Opposing Viewpoints*. San Diego, Calif.: Greenhaven Press, 1991.

Articles

Ballafante, Ginia. "Kudos for a Crusader: Jody Williams Wins the Nobel Peace Prize for her Campaign to Ban Land Mines Around the World." *Time*, October 20, 1997, p. 65.

Boulden, Laurie H. and Mike Moore. "Harvest Season." *Bulletin of Atomic Scientists*, September–October 1997, p. 30.

Chelminski, Rudolph. "The New Killing Fields." *Reader's Digest*, March 1994, p. 107.

Rogers, Adam. "Science of War, War of Science." *Newsweek*, October 20, 1997, p. 51.

Strada, Gino. "The Horror of Land Mines." *Scientific American*, May 1996, p. 39.

Wurst, Jim. "Killing Fields." *The Nation*, October 24, 1994, p. 445.

Wurst, Jim. "Ten Million Tragedies: One Step At A Time." *Bulletin of the Atomic Scientists*, July-August 1993, p. 14.

Organizations to Contact (Internet Sites)

Africare
440 R Street, NW
Washington, DC 20001
Tel: (202) 462-3614
Fax: (202) 387-1034
e-mail: Africare@africare.org
<http://www.africare.org>

American Friends Service Committee
1501 Cherry Street
Philadelphia, PA 19102
Tel: (215) 241-7000
Fax: (215) 241-7275
e-mail: afscinfo@afsc.org
<http://www.afsc.org>

Austcare
Locked Bag 15
Camperdown, N.S.W. 1450
Australia
Tel: (02) 9565-9111
Fax: (02) 9550-4509
e-mail: info@austcare.com.au
<http://www.austcare.com.au>

Canadian International Demining Centre (CIDC)
P.O. Box 86
Sydney, Nova Scotia
Canada B1P 6G9
Tel: (902) 539-2802, (888) 236-4646
Fax: (902) 539-3224
e-mail: cidc@atcon.com
<http://eagle.uccb.ns.ca/demine>

CARE
151 Ellis Street, NE
Atlanta, GA 30303-2439
Tel: (800) 521-CARE
Fax: (404) 577-6271
e-mail: infor@care.org
<http://www.care.org>

Catholic Relief Service
209 W. Fayette Street
Baltimore, MD 21201-3443
Tel: (800) 235-2772
e-mail: webmaster@catholicrelief.org
<http://www.catholicrelief.org>

Center for International Rehabilitation
351 East Huron Street, Suite 225
Chicago, IL 60611
Tel: (312) 926-0030
Fax: (312) 926-7662
<http://www.banmines.org>

Handicap International
14, Avenue Berthelot
69361 Lyon, Cedex 07, France
Tel: (33) 4-78-69-79-79
Fax: (33) 4-78-69-79-94
e-mail: handicap.international.be@infoboard.be
<http://www.handicap-international.org>

Human Rights Watch
350 Fifth Avenue, 34th Floor
New York, NY 10118-3299
Tel: (212) 290-4700
Fax: (212) 736-1300
e-mail: hrwnyc@hrw.org
<http://www.hrw.org>

Humanity Dog AB
Sandsborgsvagen 50
122 88 Enskede, Sweden
Tel: (46) 8-39-9000
Fax: (46) 8-39-9439
e-mail: webmaster@humanitydog.se
<http://www.humanitydog.se/sdafram2.htm>

International Committee of the Red Cross
19, Avenue de la Paix
1202 Geneva, Switzerland
Tel: (41) 22-734-60-01
Fax: (41) 22-730-28-99
<http://www.icrc.org>

International Physicians for the Prevention of Nuclear War
727 Massachusetts Avenue
Cambridge, MA 02139
Tel: (617) 868-5050
Fax: (617) 868-2560
e-mail: ippnwbus@ippnw.org
<http://www.ippnw.org>

International Rescue Committee, Inc.
122 East 42nd Street, 12th floor
New York, NY 10168-1289
Tel: (212) 551-3000
Fax: (212) 551-3180
<http://www.intrescom.org>

Land Mine Survivors Network
1420 K Street, NW, Suite 650
Washington, DC 20005
Tel: (202) 464-0007
Fax: (202) 464-0011
e-mail: Isn@landminesurvivors.org
<http://www.landminesurvivors.org>

Lutheran World Relief
700 Light Street
Baltimore, MD 21230
Tel: (410) 230-2700
Fax: (410) 230-2882
e-mail: lwr@lwn.org
<http://www.lwr.org>

Mine Warfare Association
7715 Lookout Court
Alexandria, VA 22306
Tel: (703) 765-1046
Fax: (703) 550-8276
e-mail: lhunt@nas.edu
<http://www.minwara.org>

Mines Action Canada
1201-1 Nicholas Street
Ottawa, Ontario
Canada K1N 7B7
Tel: (613) 241-3777
Fax: (613) 244-3410
e-mail: info@minesactioncanada.com
<http://www.minesactioncanada.com>

Mines Advisory Group
45-47 Newton Street
Manchester M11FT
United Kingdom
Tel: (44) 161-236-4311
Fax: (44) 161-236-6244
<http://www.oneworld.org/mag>

Patrick J. Leahy War Victims Fund
Office of Health and Nutrition, USAID
Ronald Reagan Building, Room 3.07 010
Washington, DC 20523-3700
Tel: (202) 712-5725
Fax: (202) 216-7302
e-mail: Lfeinberg@usaid.gov
<http://www.info.usaid.gov>

Physicians for Human Rights
100 Boylston Street, Suite 702
Boston, MA 02116
Tel: (617) 695-0041
Fax: (617) 695-0307
e-mail: phrusa@phrusa.org
<http://www.phrusa.org>

Refugees International
1705 N Street, NW
Washington, DC 20026
Tel: (202) 828-0110
Fax: (202) 828-0819
e-mail: ri@refintl.org
<http://www.refintl.org>

Save the Children USA
U.S.A. Headquarters
54 Wilton Road
Westport, CT 06880
Tel: (203) 221-4045
Fax: (203) 221-4082
<http://www.savethechildren.org>

The Diana, Princess of Wales Memorial Fund
British Red Cross Anti-Personnel Land Mines Campaign
9 Grosvenor Crescent
London SW1X 7E5
Tel: (44) 171-440-7058/7071
Fax: (44) 171-831-8933
<http://www.itn.co.uk/Britain/brit0901/090113.htm>

United Nations
Department of Humanitarian Affairs
Mine Clearance and Policy Unit
United Nations S 3600
New York, NY 10017
Tel: (212) 963-4635
Fax: (212) 963-1321
<http://www.un.org/Depts/dpko/mine>

United Nations Association of the USA (UN USA)
Adopt a Minefield
801 Second Avenue
New York, NY 10017-4706
Tel: (212) 907-1300
Fax: (212) 682-9185
e-mail: unahq@unusa.org
<http://www.unausa.org/programs/aam/adoptamine.htm>

Vietnam Veterans of America Foundation (VVAF)
2001 S Street, NW
Washington, DC 20009
Tel: (202) 483-9222
Fax: (202) 483-9312
<http://www.vvaf.org>

Index